Southern Christian University Library
1200 Taylor Rd.
Montgomery, AL. 36117

# The Counselor
# in a Changing World

### C. Gilbert Wrenn

AMRIDGE UNIVERSITY LIBRARY

American Personnel and Guidance Association
1607 New Hampshire Avenue, N.W.
Washington, D. C. 20009

102 6.5
.W698
1962

D1292379

FIRST PRINTING, 10,000, MARCH 1962
SECOND PRINTING, 10,000, JUNE 1962
THIRD PRINTING, 10,000, APRIL 1963
FOURTH PRINTING, 10,000, MAY 1964
FIFTH PRINTING, 10,000, JUNE 1965
SIXTH PRINTING, 10,000, JUNE 1966
SEVENTH PRINTING, 5,000, OCTOBER 1967
EIGHTH PRINTING, 10,000, OCTOBER 1968

Copyright © 1962, by American Personnel and Guidance Association

Permission to quote up to 500 words is granted, provided full acknowledgment is given to volume, author, and publisher. Information inquiries regarding large quotations or other use of the material should be directed to the American Personnel and Guidance Association, 1607 New Hampshire Avenue, N.W., Washington, D. C. 20009.

Printed in the U.S.A.

Single copy, $2.50
10-19 copies, each $2.00
Larger quantity rates available on request.

# Table of Contents

# The Commission on Guidance in American Schools

DAEL L. WOLFLE — Executive Officer, American Association for the Advancement of Science — Chairman

C. GILBERT WRENN — Professor of Educational Psychology, University of Minnesota — Project Director

DUGALD S. ARBUCKLE — Professor of Education, Boston University

KENNETH ERICKSON — Principal, Benson Polytechnic High School, Portland, Oregon

JOHN H. FISCHER — Dean, Teachers College, Columbia University

NICHOLAS HOBBS — Chairman, Division of Human Development, George Peabody College for Teachers

WALTER F. JOHNSON — Professor of Education, Michigan State University

SEYMOUR M. LIPSET — Professor of Sociology, University of California

GEORGE E. MOWRER — Director of Education in Charge of Guidance, St. Louis (Missouri) Schools

MERLE M. OHLSEN — Professor of Education, University of Illinois

SAMUEL A. STAUFFER — Professor of Sociology, Harvard University

IRENE B. TAEUBER — Office of Population Research, Princeton University

THELMA GWINN THURSTONE — Professor of Education and Project Director, Psychometric Laboratory, University of North Carolina

This project is supported by a grant from the Fund for the Advancement of Education and administered by the American Personnel and Guidance Association. The views expressed herein do not necessarily represent the views of the Fund or of the Association.

THE COMMISSION ON GUIDANCE IN AMERICAN SCHOOLS

American Personnel and Guidance Association
1607 New Hampshire Avenue, N.W.
Washington, D. C. 20009

# *Preface*

HOW CAN boys and girls and young men and women now in school best be prepared to cope with the problems they will face twenty years from now? The world of then will be different from the world of now, at least as different as the world of now is from the world of 1940. There will be technological and industrial changes, social changes, changes in international relations, and changes in educational methods and organization. Some of these changes will offer promising opportunities; some may pose disturbing threats. Some of the changes can be predicted; others will come as surprises. That there will be major change is absolutely certain, for we have developed a society that simply cannot stand still.

How well young people of today meet the problems of tomorrow will depend upon their skills and attitudes and their resources of mind and character. How well prepared they are in these respects is primarily the responsibility of their parents and teachers. But in their development the professional counselor can have a constructive and useful role.

It is in the context of this sober responsibility that the officers of the American Personnel and Guidance Association asked Gilbert Wrenn to look into the future of society, of education, and of the role and preparation of the professional counselor. Leaders of the counseling profession want to make their group a truly professional one, one marked by high standards of competence, rigorous standards of responsibility, and truly well-informed insight into the nature of human development and the problems of adjustment to a rapidly changing world.

This is their aspiration. The current reality is that most persons employed as school counselors are inadequately prepared to meet these rigorous standards. They are largely recruited from among persons who originally prepared themselves for one career — for example, teaching history — and who later, on the basis of meager additional training, became "counselors." The hard truth is that many school counselors have not been trained to give a student much help in finding his way in an increasingly complex world.

Thus this analysis by Dr. Wrenn. To help him in his task, the American Personnel and Guidance Association appointed an Advisory Commission, divided in membership approximately equally between professional counselors and others who could look at counseling from the outside instead of the inside. As the Commission met through long sessions with Dr. Wrenn, one of the basic questions that had to be decided was "To whom are we talking?" Counselors are a basic audience, for, as the counselors on the Commission pointed out, counselors must first come to agreement among themselves on a number of basic issues. How can counseling be most constructive? What education is necessary for a fully qualified counselor? How can he most usefully apportion his limited time among the handicapped, those with the most serious difficulties, the bright students, those most likely to respond constructively to a bit of professional help? What kind of compromises between high-level aspirations and pay-day reality are possible? Can a system be developed in which each school has a highly competent and ·adequately rewarded counselor who can serve as leader and teacher to his less experienced colleagues?

Counselors themselves must accept primary responsibility for answering these questions. But the answers must merit wider support. Thus there is also an audience of teachers, superintendents, members of school boards, and some interested parents and citizens. Dr. Wrenn has written for this audience as well as for professional counselors.

How the questions are answered is of importance to children and to society generally. If school counselors are well qualified, the students can be benefited. If they are poorly qualified and incompetent, the students can be harmed. The public therefore has a stake in the debates that will be generated by this report. Dr. Wrenn has deliberately written to provoke debate, to open the eyes of his counseling colleagues to the problems that lie before them, to attempt to get them to come to grips with those problems, and to learn how to do better what for years they have been trying to do.

A book intended to stir up such discussions should be written by an author who knows what he wants to accomplish, not by a committee that must compromise its own divergent views. Compromise will inevitably come later as counselors decide how their basic problems can best be solved, but now it is time to destroy complacency, stir up ideas, and point out issues. The book and its recommendations are therefore Dr. Wrenn's work. We on the Commission have argued with him, agreed with him, let him use us as a sounding board for trying out ideas, and occasionally some of us have disagreed with what he wanted to say. But if he still wanted to say it, it is here, for this is his book, not the Commission's. Any particularly vigorous dissent by any member of the Commission will be registered in a footnote.

If it helps counselors to come to agreement on their goals and aspirations, if it helps them to determine how to educate truly well-qualified counselors and how, through appropriate research, to determine what constitutes good counseling, we will feel well rewarded, and his professional colleagues will owe the author a substantial debt of gratitude. So will the next generation of students.

DAEL WOLFLE
*Chairman*

# *Introduction*

THIS REPORT, above all, looks to the future. It proposes a blueprint for school counseling and for school counselors that reaches into the next decade or more. It emphasizes the crucial fact that there is only one way we can continue to serve youth in the years ahead and serve them well. We must understand the new social forces that are influencing young people, as well as the rest of us — and we must learn to apply new psychological insights into the nature of the individual.

The report has been prepared for all people who work in schools — counselors, teachers, and administrators — and for those parents and interested citizens who wish to see counseling develop realistically. An attempt has been made to write clearly and simply about the need of young people for counseling help in a rapidly changing world.

The Commission recognizes that one effect of the rise of individual psychology has been a tendency to overshadow the equally important impact of social factors, and it hopes to help restore the balance in this report. Counselors must anticipate social change, not necessarily its rate and magnitude, but at least its direction. It is difficult to appreciate how swiftly things are changing. Perhaps the estimate that the sum total of human knowledge doubles every ten or fifteen years may provide some idea of what is going on. We must move fast merely to keep up with our students.

Social change is not only rapid, but uncertain and complicated. We cannot predict precisely how it will affect our values and our ways of life. The release of atomic energy is both heartening for human welfare and infinitely frightening. Faster and cheaper transportation is placing the peoples of the world in each other's living rooms overnight, and with no entry hall pause. The increasing recognition that women have much to contribute in all occupations and professions is a move in the right direction. But it will change the concept and make-up of the family in ways that we cannot foretell. Such changes pose problems but they are problems that we can meet if we are prepared to face up to the full implications of the swiftness and unpredictability of social change.

This report then opens with a discussion of *the origins of guidance services in our society,* within our concepts of children and youth. It attempts to make clear why a counselor is placed in a school, that he is there to assist children and youth with their developmental decisions, their perplexities, and their often unrealistic ideas about themselves.

Chapter 2 reports on the *nature of change in certain characteristics of society.* It opens with the presentation of a few broad influences upon social change in America, a discussion of the merits and limitations of making social projections, a consideration of inventions and innovations which might speed up some projected changes ten or a hundredfold.

Chapter 3 deals with *emerging concepts of human behavior,* broad areas of understanding in which counselors must be most knowledgeable. These are the two sides of the coin, knowledge of society and knowledge of the individual and, of course, their reciprocal relation to each other. (For many of the ideas in this chapter the writer is particularly indebted to Dr. Nicholas Hobbs.)

Chapter 4 applies these changing conditions and perceptions to a *projection of schools into the next decade.* What the counselor does is greatly influenced by the nature of his school which, in turn, is responsive to changes in the conditions of society. The school pattern of the future may take several forms and these will be outlined against the background of changes in society, in schools, and in our knowledge of behavior.

Chapter 5 presents a projection of *major elements in the school counselor's task.* Three Commission studies of counselors are examined with reference to what counselors do, want to do, believe is important for the future.

Chapter 6 describes a *condensed and re-focused guidance program* for the school of the future. Four major functions of the counselor in this program are analyzed, together with a proposal for the systematic development of a program of pupil personnel services.

The final chapter is on *the counselor, his education and his concern for himself as a person.* His functions in the society of the future, in the school of the future, and with the children and youth of the future may change drastically from those of the past. So with his competencies and his professional education. To operate in the society of the near future, the fully qualified counselor must be broadly educated and sensitive to change, more so than is always the case today. Needless to say, counselors will continue to perform at different levels of preparation and effectiveness. But, still, the best counselors of tomorrow will have to surpass the best counselors of today.

Mark Van Doren writes, "The mind adventures and the mind stays home . . . the mind of our time alternates between exploring the unknown and reminding us of the known." This report will alternate between the significant known of which we need to be reminded and adventures into the unknown. The future will at times dismay and terrify us. Some projections into the next decade or two the reader will accept reluctantly or not at all for they are much too uncomfortable.

To be remembered also, and this is no new adventure for most readers, is that man is not only technological man or economic man. He is what he is because he dreams and because he loves. It is love that supports each child during a long period of infancy in which he must learn all anew with very little aid from instincts. The child must learn from parents, from those who teach and from those who counsel, for a period of fifteen to twenty years. This is a fourth of his life span in which he must be cared for and be guided in opportunities for learning. No other creature has this period of dependence and care, and only love can make it possible.

Man loves, hates, reasons, creates his own values, and it is these that make him unique. In our report, the appreciation of the qualities of man will alternate with the projection of material and social facts into the future.

C. GILBERT WRENN

## Postscript To Third Printing

The many reactions to this book during its first year of life lead me to admonish the reader:

To remember that the book makes no attempt to describe the counseling of the present but sets goals for its development over the next decade. These goals will be achieved painful step by painful step, since change is easier to resist than to embrace.

To remember that what is projected regarding counseling in the last half of the book is based upon the cultural projections of the first four chapters. Few take issue with the cultural projections (they are in all likelihood too conservative) but are disturbed about the changes in counseling that are proposed if the psychological and social needs of youth in this culture are to be met. We cannot eat our cake and have it too — we cannot have a brave new exciting world without accepting the responsibilities that these changes entail.

In particular I would hope that those who wish to have some "feel" for the book as a whole would ponder the sections beginning on pages 4, 6, 12, 26, 50, 62, 69, 74, 96, 126, 141; the alternatives, not substitutes, proposed on page 172; the hope expressed in paragraphs 9 and 10 on pages 184-185.

C. G. W.

# CHAPTER 1—CONTENTS

# *Why Guidance?*

GUIDANCE in schools is an American phenomenon. No other country in the world devotes so much attention to the child as an individual — and to assisting children in the decisions they must make as they grow up. This is a point of fundamental significance. Schools in all societies are concerned with the transmission of cultural heritages and with the socialization of the child. But in the United States, as in any democracy, there is an additional emphasis on the individual and on his needs and desires.

Such an emphasis expresses our most deeply rooted traditions, and school counseling is part of the response to these traditions. In an analysis prepared for an institute on counseling, the anthropologist E. Adamson Hoebel has spelled out a combination of four values which dominate the American way of life. (Of course, no one of these values is in itself uniquely American.)

1. *The notion of progress.* Material and social conditions are constantly improvable. There is an unceasing ferment to develop better laws, better education and more satisfying ways of spending leisure time.

2. *A rational universe.* In general we prefer to apply the scientific method rather than to rely on chance or mysticism. In this, says Hoebel, we are exceeded only by Russia among the world's cultures. We act as if we believed that man directs his own destinies. We are a nation of doers, a people who believe in action ("there ought to be a law"), not merely contemplation.

3. *Equal opportunity.* Each person should have the opportunity to exercise his special abilities in a manner that is personally satisfying and socially useful. Among the consequences of this belief are the ideal of universal education, a distrust of authority, a fluid status system, and an intense drive to "succeed." Success is often symbolized by money, but the things money can buy may be valued less for themselves than for what they proclaim about a person's abilities and personal fulfillment.

4. *Looking ahead.* The American value system is future-oriented. The Golden Age is always something yet to be realized. We count on change, even though we may not be satisfied when we get it and tend to see real improvement as still ahead.

1

There is considerable debate about how successful or unsuccessful we are in living up to our values, but the arguments pro and con will not concern us here. The main point is that these values are the American dream, the basis of our goals and traditions. They pervade everything we do. They affect the entire philosophy and practice of our educational system.

They help account for the fact that no other teacher in the world has a more difficult task than that of the American teacher. He is asked to see each student as a distinct individual who represents the hope of continued progress in the future and who is not to be submerged in the group. The goal is to understand the various phases of development that affect the student's intellectual growth and to assist him in making appropriate adjustments and choices along the way. This emphasis is seen in both public and private schools, and at all educational levels.

To aid in this task, school counselors are employed in a substantial proportion of our American high schools and in many of our elementary schools as well. They are currently responsible for the development of a school guidance program — bringing to a student an increased understanding of the educational and vocational information essential to wise choices; utilizing psychological measurements and careful records for both teacher and counselor understanding on the one hand, and for interpretation of the student to himself on the other hand; health services for both physical and mental health needs; school social workers for providing adjustments where needed between home and school; school psychologists for assistance to teacher and student on learning tasks; assistance to the student in finding part-time and full-time jobs, etc.

Central to this program are: (1) the possession by school administrators of what is sometimes called "the student personnel point of view," a philosophy which includes an awareness of individual differences, respect for the integrity of students, willingness to let students make decisions for themselves, and so on; (2) the careful study of students and the professional help given to them by counselors; (3) the coordination of the school program and community resources by the counselor or by someone appointed to be a director of these services.

All persons who contribute to the psychological growth of the young — parents, teachers, and youth organization workers as well as counselors — work within the limits of their responsibilities. The school counselor has a unique contribution to make. He can have a perspective different from that of the parent or teacher who may know the child more intimately in certain areas of behavior. His knowledge of human behavior in general and his awareness of many other children of the same age enable him to have a comparative understanding of individual patterns of behavior. Sometimes this is a deep understanding also.

The counselor need not evaluate or judge a student's behavior as parents and teachers must do upon occasion. He is not as emotionally involved as a parent. Nor is he charged, as is a teacher, with seeing that a student meets a certain standard of intellectual growth in a given field. So, if he has the competence and the time, he can achieve a relationship free of threat and unrestricted as to scope, a relationship denied most others.

The counselor plays an important role in contributing to the student's own self-understanding and growth. The counselor's task is not to attempt to change the student directly, but to facilitate the student's own efforts toward more mature behavior. The student's life and decision are his, not the counselor's; the self-learning process is his, not the counselor's. In many respects, the best expert on the student is the student himself and the counselor must help him to become a more qualified expert — less biased, less self-deceptive, more knowledgeable. The counselor sharpens the student's sense of personal reality and broadens his horizon of present and future environments.

The school counselor's task can be seen only as the needs of children and young people are understood, for apart from these needs and the needs of the society of which they are a part, the counselor has no reason for existence.

## The American Concern for Youth

The counselor's role is one expression of our society's deep concern for the welfare of children and youth. So deep is this concern that families sacrifice themselves for their children in many ways. They go to great lengths to provide for their children the best clothing, the best homes, the best community facilities for social development and recreation, and to provide for the greatest possible protection from exploitation and social perversion. (Unfortunately much of this parental concern consists of providing things *for* children, not loving and living *with* them.) Professional people in the various human behavior fields speak approvingly of the "child-centered" home and of the democratic family in which children are consulted on all matters which affect them. Youth tends to be for many a cherished period of life, one idealized and held apart.

Some commentators regard our concern for youth and its impact on school counseling as a most hopeful and constructive development. Each generation looks hopefully to the future and provides for the next generation. There is the hope that youth will handle the social and economic problems of our culture

3

better than we have. The emphasis on children and youth is a sign of the American tradition of respect for the integrity of each human being.

Other observers view this emphasis with alarm. They consider it an example of overattention to the young. They contend that so much help and protection may weaken character instead of building a mature sense of responsibility. Young people tend to expect attention long beyond the time when they should be giving and not getting. Permitting children to do what they like to do rather than what is more difficult is seen as a serious mistake. Some observers believe that adults may feel an actual hostility toward youth, that the youthful person becomes the scapegoat for the frustrations and anxieties of the adult.

Recently a juvenile court judge compared the treatment of delinquents in the United States with their treatment in other countries. She concludes that we are harsher toward our young people, less tolerant of their behavior, in a sense more willing to blame them for our society's difficulties than is true in many European countries. We have not allowed them a "psychological moratorium" during which they can experiment without being called upon to succeed. Comparisons of Europe and America frequently lack realistic overtones, but it is possible that we do not have all of the answers regarding the treatment of youth. Certainly, critics say, many unpleasant outcomes may be attributed to our overindulgence on the one hand and our harsh criticism on the other.

## Persisting Needs of Youth

In many respects the future needs of young people will be the same as those of young people today or a generation ago. Children need security, affection, and meaningful activity. They need an understanding of the limitations within which they must operate and within which they find security. They need chances for exercising the imagination and opportunities for feelings of achievement.

As a child grows into a youth, he still needs the sense of being loved and believed in by someone. But he also needs a new sense of achievement in which there is some line of direction or growth so that he is moving somewhere, not just moving. The youth needs some understanding of and a feeling of comfortableness with the opposite sex. He develops a growing sense of independence from the adult world. Youth clings firmly to the society of his own age group and is influenced mightily by the standards and behavior patterns of his contemporaries.

Beyond this is the basic need of youth in early and later adolescence for some understanding of "who one is" and what

4

significance he has in the world. Erik Erikson calls this the adolescent's task of *finding identity*. It involves integrating childhood self-images and understandings with a changed sense of physical growth and endowment, with the new social roles of adolescence, with the driving need for feeling personally significant. There is always a danger that the adolescent will be unable to accomplish such integrations. If this happens, he may display negative identity — a dedicated attempt to become what his parents, his class, or his community do *not* want him to be. The task of discovering one's identity is more difficult for boys than for girls, and the reasons will be discussed in Chapter 3.

Children and youth are generally conformists but over the years from childhood to adolescence the focus of conformity changes from the adult world to the youth world. The youth moves from trying as a child to do what the adults think should be done to the adolescent's attempt to do what his own age group thinks is appropriate. In all of this, he is moving toward the reality of who he is but he is still vitally influenced by others' expectations of him. The adolescent is a collection of mirrors which reflect what other people expect of him. Some mirrors reflect adult expectations; some are those of his own peers. Sometimes he never gets beyond conforming to what others think he should be, and so his pattern of behavior never reflects his *own* sense of who he is. All of this is a process of identification, first with adults, then with age peers, and finally (hopefully) with his own image of himself.

The adolescent of high school age is indeed in a difficult in-between position. He is neither child nor man, frequently behaves like one while longing to be like the other; *is* like the one on one day and like the other on the next day. He is in conflict with adult society and rejects the society of childhood, so he is forced to make his own. The conflict between the adolescent individual and society does not mean war; it does not necessarily involve hostile action. But it is a time during which the adolescent differentiates himself as a person from his total culture, although eventually it must be on the culture's terms. By becoming a person in his own right, he becomes capable of adequate emotional relationships with other people in his society.

Needs growing out of this type of personality growth and cultural adjustment are timeless. They have always existed and will probably always exist. Currently, and doubtless in the future, children and youth always need two types of influence bearing on them concurrently — the limiting and the expressive. They must know both responsibility and freedom. They need to know the limits within which they are expected to behave within their society and at their age level, and at the same time to be given assistance in moving in ever-widening circles within these limits. Expression of self within some circle of limitations prepares for the larger responsibilities of the next stage of development. This seeming antithesis of restriction and freedom creates confusion with which an understanding counselor must deal.

Students need standards to which they are held, and they need counseling assistance in accepting and meeting these standards. So many situations met by a young person have never been met before. They present a strange and somewhat frightening pattern that must be understood before it can be dealt with effectively. Society sets the expectations as do the parents within the sub-culture of the family.

These expectations, in a curious sort of way, demand that children and youth live within the present culture, but that they also be prepared to live beyond it. The expectations are for both conformity and contribution. Youth must be respectful of the present social conditions and limits, but be ready to meet new conditions and demands, or to make them. Each generation behaves in this understandably inconsistent fashion. The present generation of adults is perhaps more apprehensive of marked technological, economic, and cultural changes than has been any preceding one. If they are not, they should be!

## A Sharper Focus on Some Needs

As already pointed out, the adolescent has always identified himself strongly with his contemporaries and their behavior patterns. But this tendency is aggravated in a complicated world that is becoming more and more complicated — a world where we live together in more and more tightly packed communities, while being assaulted by a barrage of worldwide social and political forces. There is a growing feeling among adolescents of being isolated from the adult world rather than being on the verge of entering it. As a reaction, they may cling even more fiercely to the members of their own generation. This is the root of the "separate society" notion, the idea of a widening gap between youth and adults.

The loneliness of the adolescent is a deep and utter loneliness, and the future may intensify it. His quest for personal identity will be more critical than ever. He will need more help than ever to find himself in a complex metropolitan community during the sixties. His problems will be more stubborn in a nation that must either quality-produce or economy-produce to keep up with rapidly developing economies in other nations, in a time when a longer period of education must be integrated with the needs for mating and marriage, in a world where early toughmindedness and sensitivity to others compete for emphasis.

The adolescent faces increasingly a world of new conditions and new opportunities, a world where occupations change as well as values. Many occupations of 1960 will be greatly modified or pass out of existence by 1970 or 1980. New occupations will appear. For example, the relationships between newspapers, news magazines, radio and television as media of communication are by no means fixed, and during this development new occupations may appear and others disappear. In another sphere, automation will change radically the entire world of business and industry. There will be fewer of the old types of jobs. Shorthand will be restricted to a few specialists or will pass out of existence. The dictation process itself, as a part of office procedure, may well be made more automatic with the dictated record being transcribed directly. The entire perception of middle management will be transformed as electronic computers are increasingly programmed to make executive decisions.

One can see the trend of things in thousands of advertisements prepared by large industrial companies, many of which did not exist a generation ago. Here is a recent example, an excerpt from an advertisement calling for job applications from persons experienced in:

The non-equilibrium population of energy levels

Phenomena at temperatures near absolute zero

Physics of very thin films

Exploration of the "room at the bottom"

Theory of adaptive machines

New concepts of computer organization

Development of exotic optical techniques

Do these areas of research sound strange to you? The world of science and technology is filled with strangeness — and it will become stranger still.

Developments in communication and transportation will also affect occupational opportunities markedly. In effect, they will put the United States border to border with other members of the international community. As far as military and economic matters are concerned, the insularity of the United States is a thing of the past. The same will soon be true in cultural matters. Opportunities for travel and for learning from other cultures will increase to an extent that would have been inconceivable during the 1930's.

So the occupational outlook is assuming an increasingly international aspect. Although the great majority of jobs will, of course, be in this country, more and more young people will have jobs abroad. They will need and want the kinds of cultural knowledge which will prepare them to pursue careers most effectively in other nations. They will have to learn what it means to live and work in a community several thousand miles beyond the boundaries of the United States. In all these things important help can come from the counselor who has made special efforts to understand worldwide social change.

It should be pointed out that social change will affect adults perhaps even more deeply, including counselors and other adults who must deal with youth. Today's children have been brought up in a world of television, atomic bombs, jet planes, and the threat of totalitarianism. Acceptance of this world picture is no task for them; it is all they have known. They find it easy to live with the concept of space flight, 2,000-mile-an-hour airliners, transmission of television on a worldwide basis, automation in all forms, and the speeding up of our society's adaptation to continuing international tensions. Not so for many adults who were born in the days of Model-T Fords and national isolationism.

Many adults of this generation find it difficult to accept rapid change. They are hard pressed to understand and adjust to conditions which youth regards with unconcern. Adults born and reared in small communities or open country find the increasing concentration and complexity of city life confusing and threatening. Far fewer of the young people of the next decade will have experiences of this order. Three-fourths or more of them will be born in large cities and will take metropolitan living for granted.

The counselor's task is correspondingly complicated. It is not enough for the counselor to understand youth in isolation, as it were. More than ever before, the counselor must understand not only the student but himself and his adult contemporaries as they attempt to adjust to a rapidly changing technology and world order.

8

# *New Directions in American Society*

# CHAPTER 2—CONTENTS

# *New Directions in American Society*

IT IS obvious that our society faces a complex of new situations and intensified change. Some of the changes ahead are as exciting as a novel of the future. Some are most uncomfortable to contemplate. Consider some of the projections into the future from a 1960 seminar of the National Education Association on societal issues in the 1960's that will affect American education:

> Re-emphasis upon achievement and excellence will become more evident, largely as a reaction to the Communist challenge.
>
> The rights of minority groups, especially the Southern Negro, will continue toward the ideal of complete legal and political equality.
>
> Increasing political responsibility and power will be transferred to larger units.
>
> The national emphasis upon material comfort will continue, and probably increase, partly because the national economy demands it.

And there were statements involving the nature of stresses that will act upon us:

> The desire for personal security will increase, sometimes at the expense of individualism.
>
> Social pressures for conformity will increase — resulting in less sympathy for an individualism that seems neutral or contrary to actions advocated by national leaders.
>
> The uncertain future will tend to promote a "pleasure in the present" philosophy.

Notice the conflicts here between individualism and conformity, between an increasing desire for security and an increasingly uncertain future.

This chapter discusses some of the major elements of social growth in the decade ahead. More specifically, it discusses those elements which may be expected to exert strong influences upon the development of young people and schools, those which will determine the counseling needs of youth and the sort of knowledge the counselor must have. The following elements are selected for particular consideration.

Southern Christian University Library
1200 Taylor Rd.
Montgomery, AL. 36117

1. The pressure of populations
2. Jobs in the future
3. The changing family
4. Clustering together
5. The growth in wealth
6. The impact of federal government
7. The world next door

*Broad Influences upon Social Change*

But before considering these points in detail, we should consider the major factors which influence all social change in our country. Some of these are contrasting. We believe in material progress, in new things, but also we devoutly believe in *people*, their rights, their freedom of choice, their education. Education is a big thing in our country — few countries have gone further in approaching universal education, in translating individual rights into informed freedom and informed opportunity. To be educated — partly the label, partly the urge to know — is the universal dream. Schools are very influential, will be more so because there is so much more to be learned just to keep pace with what is known. There is a danger here — we must not confuse amount of education with human worth.

Some influences are relatively new and very powerful of which perhaps three should be mentioned — the *scientific mode of thought*, the *search for a sense of direction*, and a *sense of nearness to the rest of the world*. Since our relations with other nations are to be treated later in this chapter, it need only be said here that many persons find the "small world" idea frightening. We can no longer be cozily isolated on our own continent. We are thrust into such close relationships with other peoples that we may feel ill at ease and not always know how to behave. Who could have foreseen in 1950 what is happening today in the United Nations General Assembly?

The search for purpose is both national and personal — perhaps the one within the other. It is as though a family had gone through its physical growing stages, had a home and income, had children who were now half-grown and who were asking, "What's it all about, Pa?" We are uneasily aware that we have grown very fast, have our feet on solid economic and democratic ground, but can't see the next steps clearly. Perhaps we can never see too clearly ahead, but we must try. And the search is a pervading concern, symbolized nationally perhaps by the appointment in 1960 of President Eisenhower's Commission on National Goals. Science is giving us an increasingly complete description of our world but it does not give us the meaning of such a world or of man's place in it — and we search for meanings.

The most pervasive of all perhaps is the great influence of the scientific mode of thought. All the technological advances that are reshaping the world are based upon the work of investigators whose tools are careful observations, controlled experiments, and disciplined thought. But science, of course, is more than technology. The scientist is an adventurer and a creator. He searches for truth — the hidden beauty — as does the artist or the poet. He takes bold steps forward but then, unlike the artist or poet, he pauses to prove them. He thinks in terms of how little we know, not how much. He realizes that no generalization can be drawn from a single incident no matter how dramatic, that probability, not finality, is the ruling law of nature, that "truth" is a tentative thing.

These notions are often strange to the nonscientist. But he is influenced by them without realizing it, and he will be more strongly influenced in the future. The realization that scientific truth is not absolute means that all decisions based on such knowledge share a fundamental uncertainty. This is difficult to live with. We like certainty but we find that all knowledge is timebound, that what we now know will be replaced by new knowledge. We find also that learning is impossible without the sacrifice of some cherished beliefs. This too is hard. Some would go no further than contending that faith is essential but must be directed toward those elements of existence which are not subject to objective proof. Some would go further.

Technological developments that are built upon basic research, of course, are far more familiar than its philosophical implications. These developments are in the imminent future:

> The fuel cell, a cheap and efficient device which converts fuel or heat to electricity with no moving parts. This device would affect heating, lighting and propulsion. It might even bring about individual flight by means of a rocket belt. Transistor radios may be powered from the heat of the human body.

> Artificial photosynthesis, applying on a mass-production basis the process by which plants build their tissues out of air, water, and sunlight. Malnutrition and famine might be conquered if we learned to produce food "in the test tube."

> Reliable and inexpensive oral contraceptive which might play a major role in plans involving birth control as a national policy.

> Controls for what is now known about producing rain and suppressing hail, "steering" hurricanes by strategically placed explosions, even the creation of warmer temperatures when and where desired.

Reaching remote points in the solar system within a relatively short period, first with robot instrument systems and later with manned vehicles.

The establishment of communication with intelligent life on the planets of other solar systems in our galaxy.

The use of reflector satellites which will move in orbits 20,000 miles or more above the earth's surface and, among other things, serve as relay stations for worldwide television networks.

Electronic computers to help index, abstract, file and retrieve scientific literature which is being produced at an estimated rate of sixty million pages a year. (Available as early as 1960 was electronic translating of foreign languages at the rate of 1,800 words a minute, accompanied by electronic indexing of the material translated.)

Directed mutation — the use of drugs, radiation, and other means to modify man's hereditary characteristics.[1]

Important developments in any one of these areas — as well as in the social sciences — could produce dramatic, far-reaching, and unpredictable changes in society. The rate of invention in the United States is accelerating with 52,000 patents granted in 1959 against 38,000 in 1950. In this writer's opinion any one of the above advances could take place within the next 1 to 20 years. Furthermore, the next generation may well bring even more significant developments which no one can even dream of now because we do not know in what direction to anticipate.

So a warning is in order: beware of taking too literally any projections in the following sections, for any of them may be drastically modified by the social impact of discovery. Beyond this, however, let us not be intimidated by the enormous scope of impending change. It is frightening, but we must get used to it. Pascal once said something like this: "That which is known is like a circle pushing against the unknown. The larger the circle of knowledge the greater the awareness of the unknown." Such an awareness may at times be so overwhelming that we must rush back to the center of the circle, as it were, to reassure ourselves and to gain courage enough to face outward once more toward the ever-widening perimeter of the unknown which is becoming known.

---

[1] In general these developments, and the total projections of the chapter, are to be considered as a conservative estimate. Several scientific and technological developments, presented as projections when the first draft of the report was written in the summer of 1960, were on the drafting board or were being field tested in the fall of 1961!

*Dreams and Projections*

Many writers have tried their hands at surveying the sixties and looking ahead. Some have been optimistic about the United States of the near future (1970 or 1980); others have "viewed with alarm." A pleasantly wishful projection might see us as follows: We are a powerful and respected member of a world federation of nations. The vast natural and human resources of Africa, Asia, and South America are developed for world trade, intercultural cooperation, and global welfare. Our cities are bigger than ever but well organized and attractive, and surrounded by self-contained suburbs contributing in a positive way to the educational and cultural life of the community. Education through college free to all, a work week of 20 to 25 hours, leisure time that is used for recreational and creative self-expression — so the dream goes.

Although none of these visions is impossible, the broad pattern seems unlikely to be realized within a decade or two. But technological and social developments take place with startling rapidity. Who in 1940 would have predicted ICBM's and satellites, problems of radioactive fallout, the West Berlin dilemma, China's economic development, the explosion of small nations in Africa? And it would have been difficult in 1940 to predict a 1960 gross national product in the United States of $503 billion, a population increase of more than a third, or a projected world population increase of more than 50 per cent from 1950 to 1975.

A projection is neither a dream nor a prediction of actual conditions for a given year. It is rather an estimate of likely conditions made under specified and reasonable assumptions and existing trends. Most of the projections studied in preparing this report, for example, assume no major war, no upset in the relations between major powers that would involve our total economy, and no depression of the extent of that in the 1930's. We also assume continuance of the present pattern of population change, the same or an increasing rate of technological advance, and continuance of a variety of economic and social developments that are already in progress in the United States. If any of these assumptions prove faulty, all bets are off.

## The Pressure of Population

A United Nations study predicts that the world's population, which has almost doubled from 1900 to 1960, will *more* than double again by the year 2000, will soar from its present level of almost three billion to over six billion. This raw fact has enormous and frightening implications. The implications take on an even more nightmarish quality when these estimates are seen to be almost surely underestimates. For they are based on present birth rates and death rates, and it seems very likely that in many parts of the world death rates will decrease more rapidly than will birth rates. Antibiotics and insecticides are likely to be more rapidly accepted and used in death control than will effective methods be accepted for birth control. The average mortality of the less well-developed countries has been reduced markedly in recent years with one striking example being Ceylon, where the use of DDT reduced the death rate 34 percent in one year. Ceylon's population is now increasing fivefold in one life span.

"Millions and billions" of people is a meaningless phrase. Its significance cannot be grasped. No one can really grasp the fact that the nearest star is 24,000,000,000,000 miles away or that a remote galaxy is receding from us at the rate of 90,000 miles a second. One expects astronomical figures to be "astronomical" but human beings are not stars and they are *here*, not far away. Furthermore, these expanding populations are composed of people who love, have aspirations for the better things, work until they are exhausted, have fears and sorrows just as you and I. The significant difference is that, unlike you and me, most of them are born to a life of constant hunger.

It is important for both reader and writer, both student and counselor, to understand that these growing millions of people will influence our life greatly in the next decade or two. As the gap between numbers of people and amount of food becomes greater the pressure upon the "have" nations becomes heavier. We must live with this pressure, do something about it. Right now the signs are there as clearly to be seen as the rising waters along a river bank before a flood. And they have been there for some time. Food production per person was 10 per cent less in Asia in 1958 than in 1938, in Latin America 3 per cent less.

The average American eats almost twice as much per day as the average Asian, several hundred calories a day more than the European. America can support its immediate population increase with plenty of reserve. For example, we have 2 cultivated acres per person compared with Western Europe's 0.9 of an acre, Asia's 0.5, Japan's 0.2, and we cultivate these acres far less intensively than we might, growing only 4,500 calories daily per acre, compared with 7,500 in West Europe and 13,000 in Japan. The swelling population in the United States means more inconveniences — bigger five o'clock traffic jams, longer trips to work, waiting lines in restaurants and theatres. In a large part of the world it means more hunger, more death.

*The Swelling Tide in the United States*

The current annual rate of increase in the United States (a combination of birth rate, death rate, and immigration) is larger than most people realize — larger than the annual rate of increase in India, Japan, or Italy. This results in an anticipated growth in the United States which means less to us in terms of food than in terms of homes and schools. If present trends continue, we will increase 80 million in population between 1960 and 1980, more people added than constituted the total population of this country in 1900. This means that we must build at least as many houses and provide as many schools and teachers in these *two* decades as were produced in the preceding four and one-half decades. Of course, we must provide even more school facilities because the proportion of children 5 - 17 years of age attending school has increased from 69 per cent in 1910 to 94 per cent in 1960.

Why does this have meaning for the counselor? Well, it means more students who live closely together, who have to fight harder for a sense of personal identity, who have to prepare more carefully for the rapid changes that will take place. It means preparation of these students for the conflict brought about by the presence of more people who will be competing for the available houses, jobs, and recreation spots. If the counselor is employed in a city school the greater complexity of life is at once apparent. If in the rural area, it means a changed countryside with super-highways cutting through farm lands, tourists and empty beer cans in places that were once private, town meetings which now concern themselves with zoning laws and sewage costs, parents who are partly in the city and partly in the country. In either city or country, more neighbors and more complexity, more people with whom both students and counselor must learn to deal.

It also means that population growth during the next decade will be most rapid among the age groups that are not economically productive or self-sufficient. There will be a doubling of the number in the age group 14 to 17 between 1950 and 1980, a fact of considerable significance to schools and counselors. Of even greater significance is the fact that those reaching age 18 will be 50 per cent greater in 1965 than in 1960 (3.8 million) and that about this number of 18-year-olds will appear every year thereafter for at least the next 10 years. (The peak birth rate of 26.6 per cent per 1,000 population of 1947 has been followed each year by rates of 25 per thousand and over.)

Of a lesser magnitude but in the same category of the so-called non-productive groups, there will be an increase of 563,000 in those reaching 65 in 1980 over the number who reached age 65 in 1950. This is an increase of almost 50 per cent.

While these large increases are taking place, the number reaching 45 will be approximately the same in 1980 as it was in 1950. In fact, in 1970 there will be 200,000 less workers aged 35 to 45 than in 1960. This is, of course, a result of the low birth rate of the 1930's.

The increase in numbers of the younger and of the older throws a heavy burden of productivity upon those in the middle ranges. This has been the situation for generations, but the load is getting heavier. It is true that for those 65 and above productivity energies and opportunities will doubtless increase. This will be offset, however, by a necessarily longer period of education for the young, an education required by the increasing demands of a technological and socially complex world of work.

## The Meaning for America

The most vivid population development of which counselor and student should be aware, however, is the distance between the "comfort ratio" of the increased millions in the United States and that of the increased billions in the rest of the world. We are currently the ultimate among the nations having the comforts of life, and the gap between us and the "have-not" peoples is likely to increase. It is even now a very critical gap. Mathematician J. D. Williams describes it in this manner: The earth is pictured as a partly flooded cellar 25 by 25 feet with about one-fourth of the floor dry. The American enjoys the use of a 6 by 2 foot dry spot, but there are 15 other inhabitants of the cellar, all armed and two-thirds of them incredibly poor and hungry. The American has about half of the food and the other goodies in the cellar and has his attention fixed on these. He is not particularly aware of the other 15 inhabitants, of their arms, or of their hunger because he is not aware of the fact that his geographic isolation has vanished. He still thinks of himself as occupying a distant part of a limitless earth although in reality he is in the middle of a very limited cellar.

The growth of the world's population has grave implications for American youth and their education. Numbers of peoples and discrepancies between cultures are not fancies but facts. Our best brains and our most elevated values must be combined in meeting the survival and self-respect needs of these vast peoples and in effecting some resolution of the discrepancies. There is a strange inconsistency in our willingness to help other nations fight disease and reduce the death rate but our apparent inability to assist them at the other end of the life continuum. We assist them in death control but not in birth control. There is little chance for a society to improve its standard of living unless one control is balanced against the other.

18

This is a task scarcely recognized by this generation, to be attacked by the next generation and the ones succeeding it. Its presence must be seen by legislators, parents, teachers, and counselors. Without this, planning for the guidance program of the *future* may prove futile indeed.

## Jobs in the Future

The Automation Revolution is changing the occupational structure fully as drastically as did the Industrial Revolution. The major difference is in the elevation of the brain power required. The machine operator is being replaced by the designer, installer, maintenance man, programmer for the automatic machine and electronic computer. The electronic specialist who installs or maintains computers, for example, must be a person with intensive training requiring a higher degree of abstract intelligence than was expected of the expert machinist in pre-automation days.

The electronic computer with its thousands of operations per second, its memory bank capable of storing millions of items, its feedback loop which permits it to review its own work and improve its own performance is still not replacing the brains of man. In no remote sense is this true. Man designed the computer and man must program into it whatever he gets out of it. It can do some things infinitely faster than man and more accurately. For example, the computations necessary for building the St. Lawrence Seaway would have involved all Canadian human computation resources for a period of 20 years. One computer did the job in 500 hours, and it could now be done in less than 100 hours. The increase in computer speed over the past 10 years has been projected by one company to 1970 with the startling finding of computer speed on that date being approximately equivalent to the speed of light.

Occupations in industry and business will eventually all be changed by our use of automatic, self-correcting machinery and electronic computers. Not only must the maintenance man and programmer be intelligent and specialized but the machine tender or operator must be a person who is steady and dependable beyond what is expected of the present-day artisan. He may have less to do but the assurance that this will be done and at the right moment places heavy responsibility on the person involved. One operator controls a complex segment of an industrial operation and failure to live up to responsibility carries a far greater cost factor. The analogy with the radar operator on a combat ship in wartime is perhaps appropriate, one whose eyes were fixed constantly on the screen watching the pips. But the automatic machine worker does not operate under wartime discipline, nor on two-hour shifts.

It is clear that the counselor who helps the student think in terms of those changed conditions cannot depend upon his own vocational experience or the accumulated experience of his generation. "Experience" is of less importance as the rate of change accelerates and the past more rapidly becomes the remote past. Fathers have always had difficulty in convincing children that they should learn from his, the father's experience. And they will have more difficulty in the future. So with the counselor. He must not reason upon the vocational experience of his generation. He can help students only upon the projected conditions and terms of the future — the future which is almost the students' present. The counselor must think *future* and not experience or he will be of diminishing value to the student of the sixties and seventies.

*Occupational Trends*

Counselors know, of course, that during the 1950's some sort of a sound barrier was broken when "white collar" workers began to outnumber "blue collar" workers. Our pioneering industrial society moved in the direction of a new kind of pioneering. This has little to do with income since many production workers have a considerably higher income than office workers or even people in professional fields such as teaching or counseling. But the preponderance of *the kind* of work has shifted. Such a movement will continue into the next decade as suggested by the fact the service industries (commerce, transportation, government, professions, personal service, etc.) are projected to increase 25 per cent during the sixties and production industries only 14 per cent.

Figures from a 1960 Department of Labor bulletin provide a projection for still another classification of occupations.

### Estimated Change in Employment 1960-1970

| Occupation | Per cent Change from 1960 to 1970 |
|---|---|
| Professional and technical workers | + 41 |
| Proprietors and managers | + 24 |
| Clerical and sales | + 27 |
| Skilled workers | + 24 |
| Semiskilled workers | + 18 |
| Service workers | + 25 |
| Unskilled workers | 0 |
| Farmers and farm workers | − 17 |

"By far the greatest growth will be in the professional and technical group — particularly engineers, scientists, and many kinds of technicians. Additional large numbers of teachers, nurses, and accountants will be needed.

"Within the proprietors, managers and officials group, the rate of growth will be much greater for the executive and managerial group in business than for the proprietors of small enterprises.

"Despite the advances in automation in record keeping, the increasing volume of paper work will result in an increasing demand for clerical workers.

"Among manual workers, the most skilled groups will show the most rapid growth — particularly large increases are expected among building trades craftsmen, mechanics and repairmen, and machinery workers. The number of unskilled workers will not increase in the years ahead."

These are rather broad classifications, suggesting abstractions rather than the activities of people. Agriculture, for example, is exciting not because there is a declining number of those employed on farms, but because agriculture is the scene of the greatest technological revolution in this country. If by "farming" one means making one's living directly on the farm, then perhaps only one in ten of the boys now growing up upon farms will make their livelihood as farm operators. But if one looks at agriculture in all of its economic and technological implications — machinery, fertilizer, distribution, accounting, a wide variety of research, etc. — then millions more must be included. Even farming is increasingly large scale and technical in operation, requiring education and technical knowledge of a substantial order.

As suggested earlier, business vocations are changing drastically in response to various forms of automation. Business will demand more general managers, men or women who are comprehensive in interests and competent in large-range planning. The machines can do much of the executive work. Most frequently in business the educated and the teachable will be preferred to those having the "up through the ranks" kind of experience alone. The use of computers requires a preciseness of decision and an anticipation of outcomes that will demand more from management rather than less. While one management forecaster predicts that computers will soon take over much low level executive decision-making, another insists that computers make brains, high-level and planning brains, far more important than ever.

The development of information technology makes bigness in business no longer a handicap. During World War I, reports of an inventory of military material were received in Washington about two weeks behind the day. In World War II, these data were reported twice a day. Fourteen years later a business can collect almost instantaneously a tremendous variety of data from a great many sources, have them analyzed and put into report form at the rate of 600 lines a minute. In 1960 a large airline announced an IBM installation that would make it possible to secure information within nine seconds on seat reservations from 1,200 points in the United States.

The most obvious shift in the occupational structure is the demand for professional and technical workers. Note that their projected growth during the sixties is 50 per cent greater than that of the next fastest-growing group. It is estimated that by 1970 there will be 550,000 scientists and almost one and one-half million engineers employed in the United States, nearly double the number of either currently employed. (The employment of scientists and engineers in industry increased seven per cent in the single year 1959.) College teachers too must increase their present number of 200,000 by about one and one-half times by 1970 if demands are to be met. Similarly, it is believed that semiprofessional technicians such as engineering aides and electronic specialists will by 1970 be nearly double the 700,000 estimated to be employed in 1959.

A revolution comparable to that of automation is the employment in non-academic vocations of people prepared in the natural sciences and the social sciences. Government, business, and industry now want professional people of all sorts from anthropologists to zoologists. In 1960 - 1961 the number of mathematicians wanted in business and industry exceeded the supply. The same was said for economists, both professions that until a few years ago were largely restricted to academic employment. Within a wide range of fields, academically prepared people can follow their vocation in either an academic or a non-academic setting.

*Education and Jobs*

It is obvious that from decade to decade a longer period of formal education is going to be required in most vocations. Required too will be frequent retraining on the job, or even re-education toward a new vocation, as occupations change rapidly within themselves and new occupations develop. What should worry counselors in this connection is the estimate of the Department of Labor that if *present trends continue*, seven and one-half million new labor force entrants during the next decade will not have completed high school. One-third of these (two and one-half million) will not have completed the eighth grade. Vocational planning for them will be difficult in the face of a diminishing number of vocations which call for less than a high school education.

It is true that the *proportion* of 18 - 19-year-olds attending school are projected to increase from 41 per cent in 1960 to 50 per cent in 1970 for the boys and from 30 per cent to 34 per cent for the girls. Similarly the proportion not having completed elementary school is projected to drop from 18 per cent in 1960 to 9 per cent in 1970. Still the *numbers* without such completion are distressingly high and suggest employment and social problems of large proportions. School dropouts experience more unemployment and get lower-level jobs than do high school graduates, partly of course, for the same underlying reasons. School administrators and school counselors up and down the line must move to see: (1) that students capable of high school graduation and beyond are identified early and individually motivated to continue to their optimum educational level; (2) that students easily discouraged in academic work are given as meaningful an educational experience as possible; (3) that potential dropouts for whatever reason in both elementary schools and high schools are prepared for vocational entrance; (4) that continuation education is provided for early school leavers who discover through experience their need for further part-time or full-time school work.

One of the knowns of which we must be frequently reminded is that from 1960 on those who "have" (education) "get" (the better jobs). No other single factor will be as important for labor force entrants as the level of education they have attained. For the professional and technical occupations it will be the kind of education as well as the amount but for most it will be the amount of *what they have learned generally about the world, themselves, and the skills of communication.*

*Population Changes and the Labor Force*

The discussion in the preceding section of population developments in the United States has immediate significance for the nature of the labor force during the 1960's. Almost nine-tenths (88 per cent) of the labor force to be added during this decade will be men and women under 25 and over 45 years of age. The middle ranges will see very few additions as a result of the low birth rate during the 1930's and early 1940's. On the other hand, young people under 25 will be added in large numbers and will constitute nearly one-half of all the additions to the labor force during that decade. The 26 million young people entering the labor force during the 1960's will provide by far the largest task of vocational counseling, placement, and on-the-job training that this country has ever experienced.

The narrow-waisted appearance of any graph showing the age distribution (flaring out at younger and older age levels and narrowing in at the middle-age levels) will be prominent during the 1960 decade but it will not last throughout the next decade. It will have been pushed up into the next age level. By 1980

23

the 26 million who will have entered the labor market during the sixties will have filled out the narrow waist and will give the entering workers of 1980 a hard run for their money. And the young workers will be there in abundance by 1980 because the birth rate has remained almost constant for the past decade and a half. For a good many reasons the next decade and a half will see strong competition for all but the top ranking jobs and many young people must be prepared for the inevitability of not getting what they want.

*Women in the Labor Force*

It is no longer a man's world — that is, the paid occupational world. It has never, of course, been "a man's world" in more than a fair half of the important attributes of mankind. In 1970 there will be about 30 million women workers in the United States, more than one-third of the total of all workers. This will be an increase in the number of women workers of 25 per cent over 1960 as compared with an increase of 15 per cent in men workers.

Some of the 1970 increase, to be sure, will be in the nature of part-time work. Of the almost four million increase in part-time workers in 1970 over 1960 the majority will be younger workers in school but many will be women whose children are in school. The tendency for young married women to work outside of the home became sharply apparent during the war years but continued throughout the fifties. There are many reasons — the mother is still young and active; the modern home has many conveniences to shorten the hours of housework; early marriages send children to school while the mother is yet in her twenties; there is a lack of participation in community life which too often accompanies movement to urban centers; women learned during the war that they could work outside and keep up a home.

Most important perhaps is the fact that they are needed in the working world. It is this last influence that will call more women into the labor force during the sixties. There will be a shortage of male workers in the 30 to 45 age range, and married women are an excellent source of supply. An employer will make the adjustments necessary if he needs intelligence and young maturity badly enough. Two part-time workers are not as easy to arrange for and supervise as one full-time worker but it is also possible that two capable but distinctly different workers may bring more new ideas and vigor to the job than one full-time person.

*Attitudes Toward Women Working.* The fact that so many women now work full time or part time requires some adjust-

24

ment in attitudes on the part of both men and women. A generation ago women workers were a young group and were unmarried. Men are still reluctant to admit women to some vocations — and women are often reluctant to re-interpret their perceptioṇ of the feminine. At least two attitudes have been pretty largely changed — women are as "bright" as men in any characteristic to be named, and the home and children do not necessarily go to pot if a wife and mother works part time. Today the average age of women workers is 40 (it will be well over 40 by 1970), and the majority of them are married.

Women must be considered an important labor source for they have at least half of the brains of the country, and brains are badly needed. Many curious rationalizations are offered to justify a belief that women are not as intrinsically competent in mathematics and science as men. In the elementary school where cultural attitudes toward women have not yet had an influence, girls do as well as boys in these subjects. Few women enter these fields, to be sure — in the United States only one per cent of the working college graduate engineers are women and only 11 per cent of the scientists. But this is an attitude restriction not an aptitude one. Else how explain the fact that in Russia at least 50 per cent of the professional people generally are women and 20 per cent of the engineers? (Comparisons are hazardous for "professional" and "engineer" mean different things in different cultures. The figures still are striking.) The same attitude restriction doubtlessly affects the flight of women from the graduate schools, discussed in Chapter 4.

By 1980 we may look with bewilderment upon the 1960 attitude that women are restricted in their occupational choice because they are women. Counselors and teachers contribute to this restrictive concept almost as much as do parents (and of course they are now influencing the young women of 1975). "This isn't a good field for you because you're a girl." "Of course you want to marry and have a family" (implied). "Don't take your vocational choice very seriously." Such attitudes show ignorance of facts and deny to the girl the same integrity of choice that is defended for the boy.

*Negroes in the Labor Force*

A second expanding source of labor for the 1960's is the Negro population. It is perhaps needless to comment that Negro workers are not being used to their fullest capabilities because of racial discrimination and lack of education. In spite of substantial efforts upon the part of hundreds of communities the Negro is still low on the educational totem pole. Recent Census

Bureau data indicate that while 80 per cent of the white youth 14 - 17 years of age are attending school, this is true for only 65 per cent of the Negroes in the same age group. The school integration confusion of the past few years will have served a valuable purpose indeed if it has focused the attention of all America upon the educational needs of Negro children.

It is certain that during the next decade increasing proportions of Negro children will complete high school. An increase is expected too in the proportion who attend college. With increased education the utilization of the Negro in the upper levels of the labor force will follow naturally for the second handicap to the Negro, racial discrimination, is being attacked vigorously by both public and private agencies in all parts of the country. The National Urban League and the Federal Committee on Government Contracts, for example, both report encouraging developments. During the past three years the Urban League reports such developments as the employment of hundreds of Negroes in airline white-collar jobs in New York, employment of Negroes as interstate Greyhound bus drivers, of Negro professional workers by more than 35 scientific and technical companies in Detroit, of stenographers in New Orleans, of chain store grocery clerks in Little Rock, etc.

Twenty years ago there were 21 unions in the AFL-CIO with color bars. Today there are only two with formal restrictions. Scores of national firms such as RCA, IBM, General Electric, Bristol Meyers, the majority of aircraft companies, etc., now employ on a non-discriminatory basis. The Department of Labor reports that the employment of Negro workers in professional, technical, clerical, sales, and skilled jobs has doubled in the past 20 years. The proportion of white workers in these areas is currently, however, from two to three times as great as the proportion of Negro workers, and there is still a long way to go.

*Some Further Considerations for the Counselor*

Earlier it was suggested that less and less could the counselor depend upon his own vocational experience to be of aid to the student. This means that he cannot help the student to play it safe. Nor should he. To encourage a student to be himself in his consideration of the future is to encourage him to take risks, not to play it safe. Safe and secure occupations of the present may be unsafe in the future, and the student is betrayed by such counsel.

The pressure is on for students to consider scientific occupations, and the motivation utilized is sometimes that of manpower needs, of national security. There is no doubt that the nation needs scientists and engineers and other specialists desperately, but in the long run it needs people who believe in themselves. It needs people who make their choices in terms of personal motivations and an awareness of talents possessed by them as well as in terms of contributions to be made to the national welfare. The nation needs poets and philosophers, teachers and tradesmen, bankers and bus drivers — artisans, humanitarians, and businessmen as well as scientists.

Not to be forgotten is the fact that shifts in the occupational structure will be caused by other factors than automation and general technological development. Equally clear are trends toward an increased dependence upon local, state, and federal government for many kinds of services. Whether a counselor approves of this trend does not affect the reality of many new vocational opportunities that will be opened up at home and abroad. The Peace Corps movement is scarcely to be thought of as a vocation, and yet it is indicative of action by the federal government that would not have been dreamed of a few years ago. Teaching, technical aid, and cultural study will go hand in hand with diplomacy all over the world. Our expanding cultural contacts will develop the need for such newer vocations as specialists in communication and social psychologists. On the metropolitan level city planners, economists, and engineers will be utilized in greater numbers.

As suggested earlier, services *to* people as opposed to making things *for* people will absorb an increasing number of workers. The expanding vocations include such major fields as education in all of its specializations, the health field including mental health and public health, social work including such newer fields as marriage counseling, recreation vocations, and personnel service vocations for making people more comfortable in many ways. In each of these areas there will be opportunities in both government and private business.

Research in the social sciences may develop vocations as startlingly new as some which evolve from research in the natural sciences. All of these are major movements to be studied by the counselor as he becomes culturally attuned. Changes in occupations and new occupations do not just happen. They are outgrowths of societal, technological, and scientific changes that can be at least dimly foreseen. And their nearness to the high school student of today is assured by the anticipated speed with which changes will be made.

Consideration should also be given to the lengthening life span. One might conceive of at least two periods of vocational activity, one from 25 to 50 years of age, and another from 50 to 75. The first, perhaps called the Active Stage, is characterized by physical activity, exploration, and risk taking. The second, the Judgment Stage, is characterized by less physical strain, more dependence upon judgment, some shading off in hours per work week toward the last half of the stage. There might well be shifts of vocation within either stage so that the individual should plan upon moving from one vocation to the other at the time the first considerations are being given to vocational choice. He must see change more vividly than we do because it will come upon him faster.

Margaret Mead has commented "No one will live all his life in the world in which he was born, and no one will die in the world in which he worked at maturity."

## The Changing Family

Social changes hurt worst at the family level. Parents are affected more by the changing nature of the home than are the children who know nothing else. The parent, though, is constantly trying to put new wine into old casks, to see the home in 1960 as similar to the one in which he or she was reared in 1930. The controls and aids that were used with the parent may not fit the home conditions under which their children live and they blame both themselves and "the times" when they find this out. The slow-paced home life, with focused authority and both parents present in the home for several hours per day, fits the conditions or urban, split-level living less well than it does the small-town or rural setting, particularly that of a generation ago.

It is more important than ever before that the counselor become a student of family life. If the home is so important an influence in the life of the child, and within the foreseeable future it will certainly continue to be the most important, and if the home is changing, then the counselor must keep up with the changes in order to understand and help the student. How can the counselor help Bart in vocational planning, for example, unless he knows that Bart's home is a very closely knit one in which every decision is discussed by all members of the family? With Mary the parents are "emancipated" and carefully follow a hands-off policy which avoids exercising any influence on a child's decision, a policy interpreted by Mary as "they don't care." Peter, on the other hand, is in the middle of a power struggle between father and mother and must attempt to satisfy both. Ken comes from a home where the father leaves all home and family decisions to the mother, but the mother wants the father to accept responsibility for some. As a consequence, both avoid doing anything about "school decisions." How indeed can the counselor communicate effectively with a student unless the counselor's perception of the home from which the student comes is reasonably close to the reality? He may not know *this* student's home, at least not at first, but he must know the various patterns of modern family life and the social influences that create these patterns.

*Long-term and Short-term Changes*

It seems apparent that the careful student of the family will distinguish between long-term and short-term changes in marriage and family phenomena. Long-term trends — smaller households, changing authority patterns, changing role of husband and wife — are undoubtedly related to industrialization and urbanization trends. Perhaps also these are expressions, in the social language of this period, of equalitarian and achievement values. Short-term changes are those in response to economic levels and conditions of war and peace, best typified by marriage rates and birth rates.

It seems likely that the long-term trends will not be modified easily no matter how much agitation is developed. They are *a reality to be lived with* like death and taxes. No one is going to bring back the economically integrated, self-sufficient, authority-centered rural home both because only 12 per cent of American families now live on farms and because rural families also change. Living in metropolitan areas will increase as will the proportion of married women who work outside the home. Family mobility has increased, with about one-fifth of American families reported as moving from one community to another within a single year. Many of these trends may well be a cause of concern but they are tied to long-range social changes which are likely to persist or intensify.

Short-term changes show the marriage rate and birth rate related to economic prosperity levels. Among men 20 - 24 years of age there were 27 per cent married in 1940 and 51 per cent in 1955. (The present average age at marriage for men is 22.6 years and women is 20.4 years.) The birth rate rose with the marriage rate, but the present median of between two and three children per family seems to be the result of planned family size.

Divorce in America has been on the increase since the first census in 1870, but it is related also to the short-term marriage rate fluctuations. Some wag has said that "the basic cause of divorce is marriage" and in actuality the divorce rate rises and falls with the marriage rate. This reflects the fact that 50 per cent of American divorces occur within the first five years of marriage, many within the first two years and before children arrive.

The 1955 divorce rate of 2.3 divorces per 1,000 population has fallen materially from the 3.5 rate in 1945. It is still quite high compared with the rates in other industrialized societies of the world. But so also is the remarriage rate. Three-fourths of those divorced remarry within five years and eventually 87 per cent do so. There is no repudiation in our society of marriage as such. On the other hand, writes one sociologist, we appear to be operating a type of trial marriage system in which the first marriage may domesticate both people but in one-fifth of the cases they find that they are the wrong people for each other. Certainly the *number* of divorces does not represent the number of people involved since two or more divorces may represent the same person more than once.

Another way to observe marriage and divorce in America is to compare our situation with that in other countries. In 1959 of those aged 14 to 90 a total of 68 per cent were married, 21 per cent were single (and hopeful!), 8 per cent were widowed, 3 per cent separated, and only 2 per cent were divorced at any one time. Sociologist Reuben Hill reports that an Englishman looked at these statistics and commented: "You Americans make a lot of bother about divorce but in Europe we worry about the fact that people don't bother to marry. In America 90 per cent eventually marry but in Sweden and Switzerland only 70 per cent marry and fewer yet in Ireland. The median age at first marriage in rural Ireland is almost forty."

*Balance the Picture*

Social scientists who study the family as a social institution are more likely to be aware of the total cross section of American family life than are those who have responsibility for some unhappy segment of the whole. Juvenile court judges, social workers, psychiatrists reflect what they see, and the conditions they describe are disturbing enough to be given serious consideration. At the 1960 White House Conference on Children and Youth it was pointed out that:

A half million children in the juvenile courts of America each year, 50 per cent of our youth dropping out of high school before graduation, 11 per cent of all young Americans seriously impeded by race discrimination in their search for education and jobs, 11 per cent of our children reared in broken homes, 15 per cent of our youth reared in substandard housing and poverty — these conditions represent an enormous waste of manpower and human potential which America can ill afford.

The picture seems unbalanced enough when a counselor must deal with a child from a big city "neglect" case of juvenile delinquency, where father, mother, and eight children live in two-room cave-dweller squalor. Or the student from a family where parental quarrels and separations have been frequent, addresses have changed eight times in three years, and the family is currently on the divorce docket in circuit court. Reported also by a juvenile court judge is "the 15-year-old girl back for violation of juvenile court probation, who responded to my lecture with looking me right in the eye and saying, 'But, Judge, what you don't know about me is that until I was 15 years old — nobody ever told me what to do. Nobody has ever told me when to get up or what to do, when to get dressed or what to wear, when to eat or what to eat. I've made all my own decisions myself all my life. And now, when I'm 15, you want to make rules for me to keep. Judge, I just can't do it that fast.' "

But such specialists in human problems rarely see the whole picture. Sociologists and anthropologists are less pessimistic about the American family today. They see the American family as experiencing normal growing pains, a reorganization that must follow adjustments to an urban, industrial society. Change is painful but the pain experienced does not indicate a mortal wound — only change. Sociologist Seymour Lipset proposes that belief in equality and in individual achievement are continuing and stabilizing values in our Amercan society and that in the home they contribute to present trends toward non-authoritarianism, equality in husband-wife relations, and child-centeredness which is oriented to an emphasis upon future achievement.

Reuben Hill, a sociologist who specializes in family life, agrees that the family has given up some functions but has firmly retained the basic business of reproduction, housing, feeding, and domestication of children  It may have relinquished to other social agencies such functions as formal schooling, religious instruction, medical care, and organized recreation but concentrates now on a psychological function, that of the personality development of its members. It provides "warmth, love, and sanctuary from the anonymity of urban existence, services no other agency in society is prepared to offer."

## The School Counselor and the Family

The school counselor must recognize that, whatever the facts about birth rate, family size, and divorce, there are widely varying and deeply held opinions on these topics in any community. Parents are sensitive to implied criticism of either a very small family or a large one. Either may be planned and not the result of selfishness or complacency. Counselors who come from either large families or small ones are as likely to have attached a value to the size of the family of their origin as do the parents with whom they deal. There is little evidence that a small family or large one per se provides the "best" climate for child growth. Economic capacity to support the children's social and educational needs is a factor, but so also is the love support the

31

child receives, the integrity of the family unit, and the general psychological climate of the home.

Counselors should be knowledgeable about the interrelationship of such family factors and be slow to prejudge the home and the parents. Nor can one arrive at any balanced estimate of the quality of the family unit from the student's perceptions alone. Necessarily his viewpoint is personalized and limited to his level of understanding of parental attitudes and sibling relationships. A counselor can listen much and attempt to understand deeply but he needs to be wary of coming to conclusions about a family which may deviate from his stereotype of a "good" family.

The counselor needs to understand the changing nature of the roles of husband and wife in the family. Increasingly the wife is becoming an economic partner with the husband in both spending and earning the family income. Wives have more part than formerly in family decision-making about a variety of issues. The husband too takes more part in home responsibilities that were once considered the sole province of the wife and mother.

In a study made of families at various educational and occupational status levels it was found that the middle-class family has gone furthest in bringing the husband into taking responsibility for family tasks. This group too was likely to designate more tasks as the joint responsibility of husband and wife. Families lower on the educational-occupational scale placed more of the home burdens on the mother and the children. For all classes, the majority pattern is for the wife to assume responsibility for the greatest number (40 to 50 per cent) of home and family tasks with the second more common pattern being that of joint responsibility (25 to 28 per cent). This latter pattern was most apparent for such family tasks as disciplining children, training in manners, supervising school work, deciding when to buy a new car, planning the budget, etc. Whether or not this was true in the counselor's family the shift in family roles must be understood by the counselor — the wife has a voice in the economic aspects of the home, the husband may care for the baby and do family shopping, jointly they enter into most decisions regarding the children. The counselor is likely to be overly aware of a few dominant mothers and a few arbitrary and self-centered fathers and misjudge the family pattern present in perhaps 80 to 90 per cent of the homes in his community.

The counselor needs to be particularly understanding of families with regard to family mobility, which is likely to be higher for younger families and for those whose easy acceptance into the community is likely to be slow. Studies of newcomers into urban areas indicate clearly that new families may be very lonely. This may be equally true for families moving into new communities and for those leaving the central city to move into the suburbs. The parents may be more lonely than the children in school, and their unhappiness contributes to the student's insecurity. The absence of kinfolk in the new community deprives the adults of a source of emotional support and makes the child feel more rootless. The counselor in helping the new student in school must understand the loneliness of the family from which the child comes. He might well think of a family contact as an aid to both child and family.

It is equally essential to remember that a divorce is hard on both parents as well as the children. Frequently sympathy goes to only the children. Impending divorce and the divorce itself has created in parents a choice-anxiety which is very punishing, for whichever choice is made the results inflict deep hurts. Our society is not kind to a divorced person, particularly the female of the species. Nor should a counselor "take sides," certainly not in spoken form but not even in his own thinking. Marriage counselors know that there are always two sets of claims, two stories to be heard no matter how convincing is the first story. The hurt of both parents affect the child, and the counselor is most directly concerned at this point. But his understanding and compassion should be extended to the parents as well.

## Living Together in Metropolis

People are already speaking about the existence of a latent "Megalopolis," a super city, extending roughly for 600 miles from north of Boston to south of Washington, D. C. By 1975 or 1980 this may become one continuous urban-industrial area; by the year 2000 it may extend westward as far as Cleveland. The New York metropolitan area now extends in a radius of 50 miles from mid-Manhattan, has a population of 16 million people, contains 500 municipalities outside New York City proper and embraces 22 counties in three states. With this as a starter, Megalopolis does not seem so remote.

The metropolitan area is becoming the basic population and economic unit with more significance to its boundaries than are possessed by county or state lines. It took the United States 300 years to become an urban nation. It required 40 years or so for it to change from urban to metropolitan. Our nation is fast centralizing in 175 to 200 metropolitan centers. With one quarter of the nation's people living in 10 of these areas, each center contains one or more urban cores and an increasing number of suburbs. Indeed as rapidly as the nation tends to centralize, the metropolitan area decentralizes and spills its people from the urban center to an ever-widening periphery of suburbs. The United States today can in fact be described as "a galaxy of urban solar systems."

The urban growth, which has become one of the most pronounced phenomena of our century, has changed the economic relation of the city to its surrounding territory. It was once said that "Cities do not grow of themselves. Countrysides set them up to do tasks that must be performed in central places." Geographer Edward A. Ackerman, after analyzing the extent to which farms depend upon cities both for markets and their instruments of production, believes we may now say: "In the United States of today and the immediate future the countryside is set up by the cities to do the tasks that cannot be performed in urban areas." The locus of our population and of our economy now is and will continue to be in the metropolitan area with its urban economic centers.

The phenomenon of metropolitan growth has much significance for the counselor for increasingly he will be employed in a metropolitan area. He must be aware of the growing pains of this segment of American society with which he will be so intimately involved. What happens in the area will affect both his students' lives and his own. It will also affect his paycheck.

*The Pains of Metropolitan Growth*

Some of the problems that accompany the development of metropolitan areas are only intensified versions of well-defined urban characteristics such as the many units of government within a city, traffic congestion, and burgeoning school requirements. Other conditions are an outgrowth of the metropolitan area development itself, such as public service needs that cross city, county, and state lines, redevelopment of older or blighted areas in the urban center, marked differences in tax resources and new development needs between the urban center and the newer suburbs, and complex transportation problems. Two of these — transportation needs and area government development — serve as illustrations.

*Transportation.* With whatever speed highways leading to the city are built and expressways through the city are provided, the game is a losing one. Yet truck transportation into the city is vital and truckers become as important as firemen and policemen if people are to live.

The problem most immediately apparent to the citizens, and perhaps the most critical, is daily movement in from the suburbs and movement within the central city itself. *Mass transit, particularly commuter railroad facilities*, is essential if the downtown traffic is to be relieved.

Freeways connecting the city with other regions of the country are receiving considerable attention at present. The planned national system of highways connects major regions and most metropolitan areas effectively but it may become an illustration of "too little and too late." The burgeoning population of the metropolitan areas and the increase in the number of automobiles and trucks on the highways is moving all too fast upon the heels of the expanded highway system. Resources for the Future, Inc., estimates that within present lines of development the 58 million automobiles in use on the highways in 1960 may become 230 million in the year 2000. And we think we have troubles now!

Related to transportation development is the concern of metropolitan planners with the need for suburban residents to get to recreation areas for overnight or weekend recreation. As the land around the central city is enveloped by the suburbs, outdoor recreation areas are pushed farther and farther away. Access to nearby areas and the inclusion of planned open spaces for recreation, either man-made or natural resource areas, appear to be essential if even the present quality of urban living is to be maintained.

*Government in the Metropolitan Area.* The number and variety of urban government units within a metropolitan area is bewildering. A recent Bureau of the Census study reports a total of 15,658 individual local government units in the 189 metropolitan areas of the United States, each possessing "discretion in the management of its own affairs." They include every legal type authorized by state constitution or statute — counties, townships, municipalities, independent school districts, special districts for a great variety of purposes. The New York metropolitan area alone has over 1,000 separate governmental units.

What has grown up, around, and over local government units are public corporations which have regional powers and responsibilities. Such units as the New York Port Authority, the Chicago Park District, the various transit authorities, the North New Jersey Water Supply District, etc., perform regional functions and permit residents to have access to work, water, recreation, disease protection, and the like. It would seem likely that these will of necessity become more numerous, more legally secure, and more comprehensive if metropolitan growth is to remain healthy. Both the "wholesale" phases of government covering the area (such as water supply) and "retail" phases for each community in the area (such as water distribution) call for administrative skills and technical knowledge of a substantial order. Urban and metropolitan government posts must be filled by people dedicated to urban planning and operation as a career.

35

The Municipal Manpower Commission, under a grant from the Ford Foundation, is analyzing long-range local government personnel needs and establishing criteria for careers in this field.

*Metropolitan Area Development during the Decades Ahead*

The metropolitan area of the future is seen to consist of a Central City and an Outer City, each containing two broad divisions. The Central City will contain the economic and business center of the area, will be the hub of the circle. It will be occupied by people who work in office buildings of all sorts, people working in occupations calling for face-to-face contacts, those working in the production of high quality or unusual goods, those employed in a limited retail trade. People will live in the Hub, too, but they will be residents of apartment buildings, generally older or younger people with fewer children.

Unless marked steps are taken, the outer ring of the Central City will consist of low-income housing, older buildings (which are not replaced as is increasingly true in the Hub), and older shopping establishments. It is defined less as a geographic location than an area possessing certain economic and social characteristics. There will be many children living under culturally underprivileged circumstances. Rapid turnover and low capacity for community organization will also characterize this perimeter of the Central City.

The Outer City will have two parts also, an inner ring of suburban developments and an outer ring of self-contained communities. The inner ring will be densely populated but with single family housing, new shopping centers, and new industries. Some suburbs will have developed a slum area round their hub. The outer ring will consist of relatively independent and self-contained communities, with many of them integrated around planned units of decentralized industry. These will have less complex traffic problems because of limited access highways and short-run commuter trains to the inner city.

The division of the Outer City will generally have the best chance for the development of planned social institutions that are designed to meet the long-run educational and cultural needs of the community.

There are some encouraging signs for the future in the physical patterns of some of the newer suburban developments. These include handsomely landscaped industrial areas, modern schools and attractively designed shopping areas, all of the appurtenances of communities that are combined in a fashion to reduce to a minimum the frictions and discomforts of crowded 19th century urban patterns. These suggest that beauty, order, and efficiency *can* be combined successfully to provide an inspiring setting for living in the metropolis of the future.

In spite of the generally pessimistic tone used in describing the urban center, much is under way to improve the situation. In 1960 there could be identified 699 urban renewal projects in the United States. Some of these are truly outstanding such as the superb job in hub area redevelopment being carried out in Pittsburgh. Here pedestrian plazas, open parks, new office buildings, and new cultural facilities provide an exciting new setting for a busy downtown area. Philadelphia, Minneapolis, Baltimore, Cincinnati, St. Louis, and many other cities are doing a fairly thorough job of face lifting. The cost in any one of these runs into hundreds of millions of dollars. The Lake Meadows development in Chicago and the Fresh Meadows development in the New York City area provide whole new communities built to modern 20th century standards. They suggest that an internally stable oasis in the midst of a surrounding area of decay is feasible. Such developments are enormously costly and they require a modern form of city government action — but they are possible.

## What is the Counselor's Concern with Urban and Metropolitan Development?

First of all he must know the different environments from which Central City and Outer City students will come.

*The Central City Counselor.* Central City students will have great need for understanding and encouragement, and an appreciation for the realities of life which they face. A substantial proportion will be from low-income and/or culturally deprived homes. Newspaper editor Ralph McGill, in a study for the Ford Foundation, estimates that one child of every three now in the public schools of the 14 largest cities of the country is culturally deprived. He concludes that this proportion will grow alarmingly during the next decade to include perhaps half of the school population unless active steps are taken within the community and within the school program.

A culturally deprived student is described as one who has limited opportunities for cultural growth or who is oblivious to the opportunities that are available to him. He may be a newcomer or not. He is likely to be non-responsive in the school, be indifferent to responsibility, have poor health habits. He is likely to be over-age for his grade, have a low aspiration level, be poor in basic academic skills, and have a high dropout rate. And yet he is also likely to perform better than his test data would indicate and be unaware of but responsive to cultural opportunities. McGill is describing the Central City student in particular.

The counselor of such students has a responsibility second to none for making life more meaningful to each person. This is more than a negative task of assisting the academically lame, blind, and halt but a positive one of helping such students live beyond their handicaps, recognize their capacities for growth and achievement, believe in themselves even when no one else does but the counselor.

Students in Central City schools will vary widely, of course, just as they do now in any school. The school as a whole will take adaptive steps as the character of the student body changes. The counselor, though, will be badly needed in this setting. He must see his task in such a school as a frontier task, calling for as much courage, initiative, and inventiveness as was required of a frontiersman on the westward edge of our earlier economy. He is on a social frontier of great significance to our society.

*The Outer City Counselor.* This counselor may face deprived conditions as well, particularly in an older suburb which is experiencing its decay. It is more likely, though, that he will have students who have cultural advantages and high aspirations. They may be academically adequate but feel required to be academically the best. The pressures on them may be those of over-ambition, both of parents and of themselves. Such students need understanding, too, but this time it is understanding of the high expectations of their parents and of the kinds of defenses children and young people put up against overexpectations.

Most students attending school in the suburbs will be living in small communities around the Central City, each of which is in some ways more restricted than the small town or village community in which their parents may have been reared. Each suburb is likely to develop around some economic-social culture of its own and to draw people from a given ethnic or cultural level. This means that the students attending school in a given suburban community have a much more limited awareness of other cultural groups than if they live in the Central City or a small town. The counselor must be aware of the impact of the particular community's culture upon its students and the necessity for helping students to understand their need for becoming less provincial as they move from stage to stage in their educational career and from there into the vocational world.

It would seem vital that the counselor understand the emotional forces operating within the homes and the lives of his students. Much of this can come from an appreciation of the cultural mores of his particular segment of urban society. A counselor in such settings must have a little of the understanding of the anthropologist, the sociologist, and the economist if he is to be effective as a professional person. To be optimally helpful in working with another person, a counselor must see him as a person-in-situation. The "situation" in any one unit of a grow-

38

ing metropolitan area is as complex to understand as is the psychology of the student.

## The Growth in Wealth

Economists agree that the next decade will see a substantial increase in the national economy and in personal income. The gross national product (the sum of the value of all goods and services produced) for 1970 is projected variously to be from $740 billion to $790 billion (in 1958 dollars). This is a national increase of 50 per cent over the 1960 figure of $503 billion. The increase drops to one-third when disposable income (after taxes and other payroll deductions) per person is projected. This is still substantial. However much the economists may disagree on the factors that affect an increase in national product, all agree that the next decade will bring more wealth both nationally and personally.

Economic projections vary because assumptions of the annual rate of increase in gross national product vary from use of the past 50-year average of three per cent increase per year to the projected five per cent increase discussed in the 1960 political campaign. Another way of studying economic growth is to use output-per-man-hour or productivity. This has had an average growth over the past 50 years of two per cent increase per annum. Technological developments might boost this sharply during the next decade. In a study which assumed an average of 2.7 per cent increase per year over the next 10 years, the annual output per worker valued at $6,654 in 1957 is projected to increase in value (1958 dollars) to $9,500 in 1970.

All of these projections make the usual assumptions of no world conflict on a combat basis, no depression of the severity of that which was experienced in the 1930's, and a continuation of present trends in population increase and technological development.

### The Counselor's Concern

The counselor is concerned with our national economic health because this will affect the welfare and plans of the students with whom he works. If there is to be more wealth how much of this will be channeled into publicly supported post-high school educational facilities? How much into scholarships? Or will America continue what some have characterized as a post World War II period of private opulence and public parsimony so that the financing of further education will be the responsibility of each individual family? This will have much to do with student planning.

Counselors should understand that economists do not agree on the extent to which a given factor will affect an increase in gross national product — high versus low interest rates, balanced government budgets versus deficit spending designed to stimulate increased production, reduction of national debt versus an increase in "capital investment" proportionate to increase in the national income, etc. (It is interesting to note that our national debt just following World War II was 50 per cent greater than our GNP but the ratio has been declining steadily until in 1960 it was about 45 per cent *less* than our GNP.) These differences of opinion are just that, differences of opinion or of values, differences in inferences drawn from the same facts. Thy are related to differences in the policies of different federal administrations and different political parties. We have had over the past decade an increasing GNP and an increase in real per capita income but a question could be raised as to whether this is meaningful if there are inadequate increases in such public welfare factors as education, housing, health, and the quality of urban living? Should more of the increase in GNP be channeled into expenditures for these purposes? Will so-called deficit spending to improve the quality of national life strengthen us as a people without weakening our economy?

A 1959 report of the Committee for Economic Development, *The Budget and Economic Growth,* recommends a balanced federal budget, cash surpluses to be built up during high income years, and budget increases which would involve increased taxes to be limited to defense spending and economic assistance to underdeveloped countries. This is a point of view which would answer all questions of the preceding paragraph in a consistently negative direction. It holds that a balanced budget and economic security measures are more important than any other consideration with the possible exception of national defense expenditures.

Opposed to this point of view is one which proposes that responsibility for national welfare involves responsibility for improving the quality of national life and that this is a federal concern. Its proponents hold that state and local governments, under the pressure of the population increase and concentration, cannot maintain or improve the quality of urban services without federal participation. Indeed, Economist Otto Eckstein, in the just-mentioned Committee for Economic Development report, estimates that state-local expenditures will increase by 35 per cent between 1960 and 1968 which would represent a higher rate of growth than for all projections of federal government expenditures save those labeled "very high."

The counselor, or whoever reads these pages, will be likely to feel that the point of view which he holds has not been dealt with adequately. This is doubtless true. There are many shadings of the two broad emphases that have just been outlined. The disagreement between economists is decided and sometimes passionate. Part of the disagreement is because values enter into the picture. If the counselor is to consider thoughtfully the implications of increased national wealth and personal income that will affect the school which employs the counselor as well as the student with whom he deals, then he must come to his own conclusion regarding the *purpose* of production. For what purpose are goods produced, for what are taxes to be spent, how must personal welfare be related to public or group welfare, how much should Americans be concerned about the economic welfare of the peoples of other countries? These are some of the value dimensions that determine how one feels about production and consumption, about taxes, about risk-taking in economic development.

*A Counselor Should Know Enough to Ask Questions*

Any unwillingness to arrive at some higher level of economic understanding puts him as a counselor or a citizen at the mercy of the glibbest speaker in an election campaign. He is also helpless in guarding his own economic welfare or in knowing how to give intelligent consideration to the student's future. He is a fare-paying rider on a bus who never raises any question about why it speeds up or slows down, what a change of drivers may mean, whether the bus is heading into town or country, whether it will slow down enough for him to get off at the station of his choice. Indeed, he may have no idea regarding where he wants to get off, have a rest stop, or change buses. He is being "taken for a ride" by a bus driver who must perforce use his own judgment if the rider doesn't understand enough to speak up.

Taxes are of concern to all citizens yet few follow tax discussions in Congress, state legislatures, or city councils with any understanding — few follow them at all. Taxes influence daily living, both in the nature of the taxes levied and the manner in which the levy is spent for services to the people, and yet we are inclined to dispose of the entire question by joining in the refrain that "Taxes are too heavy." *Are* they, in terms of the services received?

The counselor as a professional person concerned with the welfare of students has an obligation to *inquire*. He may inquire about the logic back of the 10 per cent federal transportation tax which originated as a World War II measure or the logic of a heavy local dependence upon real property taxes which were appropriate for an agricultural economy but are less so for an industrial economy. He may hear apprehensive statements made about the national debt increase and he needs to inquire about the basis for these apprehensions when debt is considered in relation to income. Our American counselor needs to inquire about the statements made that more public works will benefit our economy — who pays for the works and who benefits and how does this affect our total economy?

The school counselor will not become an economist or tax expert, even an amateur one. There is little danger of that! He might, however, be a better school employee if he knew something about school bonds and how they are retired, the tax advantages and limitations of independent school districts, the manner in which libraries and parks are capitalized and supported as compared to schools. These are not difficult to understand — most of us have merely been too self-conscious to inquire. As a result we are hazy about the economic implications of school growth and support. And the present economic implications of school growth will become more perplexing in the decades ahead.

Counselors must blend economic understanding with psychological insight in answering questions about the financial support of a student's further education. The economic advantages and disadvantages of educational loans should be understood as well as the psychological implications. More students by far prefer scholarships to loans but how much have they thought about the difference? Is the responsibility for repaying a loan an economic burden or a psychological asset? This may have immediate bearing upon the vocational choice made and the training required to enter that occupation.

The school counselor cannot afford to be a graduate student in psychology and a second grader in economics.

## The Changing Impact of Federal Government

It would seem that in the decade ahead there may be more open acknowledgment of the role of the federal government in providing support for social health as well as for national defense and a common monetary system. The national system of highways is as important for economic and social well-being as it is for defense. In an industrialized economy, in fact, this type of well-being is in itself very important for defense. The same could be said for our total system of education. Our intellectual strength and our social health are two of the most important weapons we have in a warfare with an opponent who uses economic and psychological weapons.

There have been marked shifts in the American perception of federal government from the decade in which the Constitution was written up to the present. Some of these have been institutionalized into Constitutional Amendments while others are merely the working concepts of legislators. Certainly the principles or values incorporated in the Constitution are timeless but *the government function and structure to achieve values must respond to changes in the structure and function of our social economy.* An agrarian society of 13 seaboard states has become an industrialized, urban society of 50 states that is spread over a considerable part of this continent. It is also a society now closer to the rest of the world than it was in 1787 by a factor of at least 100 to 1.

Eighteenth-century economist Alexander Hamilton, early in our history, insisted that the federal government had to have a hand in tariff-making, not because it was a constitutionally provided revenue device, but because the tariff had to be used by the government as a protective device for a developing American industry. This type of federal government concern was *not* in the Constitution yet Hamilton won the day. Over the years, our federal government has shown increasing concern for railroad and airline development through land grants or operating subsidies, for the conservation of physical resources, for the protection and stimulation of industry — all of these and others dealing with the physical aspects of our economy. It has also dealt with the human factor in the form of child labor laws, stimulation of vocational education, and land grants to universities. It seems reasonable to suppose that as our society matures the federal government will increase its concern for the quality of life made possible in our society. As the physical undergirding of society has been assured, the government has been turning its attention to such social factors as health, education, employment, and life under urban conditions.

No implication should be drawn, however, that the opposing point of view lacks vigorous supporters. Senator Barry Goldwater's 1960 book, *The Conscience of a Conservative,* makes very clear that he would withdraw the federal government from all concern with education, housing, social welfare, agricultural support, urban redevelopment, and the like, as well as abolish the graduated personal income tax. He would drastically reduce the size and operation of the federal government. However much one may respect his convictions on either foreign or domestic issues it seems apparent that the tide of the times is in opposition to Goldwater's point of view, not in support of it. In 1959, for example, the normally conservative Committee on Economic Development found "federal supplementation of state and local funds necessary for the improvement of schools in the poorer states." The members of this 50-man committee differed on the kind of aid (restricted to building grants or for general operation) and on the coverage of the states (all states or only the economically poorer ones) but the

43

principle was clearly accepted and a formula presented for providing some $600 million of educational aid.

## The Counselor and His Government

The counselor may prove to be a naive economist, and he may need to work constantly at becoming a better student of world affairs, but above all he must be an intelligent citizen of our nation. This means understanding the characteristics and responsibilities of local, state, and national citizenship and acting intelligently with regard to them. If he is to counsel students whose lives are deeply affected by educational and other services provided by community, state, and nation, he must attempt to understand the changing relations between these units. Beyond this, the public school counselor is a local government employee as well. He must know the changing character of his employer at a national level.

An earlier section suggested why a counselor should know his urban government, and a later one will deal with why he should be vitally aware of the closeness of America to the rest of the world. In between these comes his concern for the federal government. He will hear much discussion during the next decade of "federal aid to schools" and he should refrain from being a partisan in the argument merely because he may benefit economically. What safeguards should be developed against overdependence of the local government upon state and federal government? There are legitimate concerns of state and federal agencies for the welfare of community schools, both public and private. How identify and defend these without losing the appropriate degree of local autonomy? When does "local" mean the best interests of his students and his community and when does it become limiting and damaging? Is the federal government dangerous when it contributes support but does not specify content? Or is this combination possible — either explicitly or implicitly?

*Some of the Issues.* The boundary line between federal and state functions in our interdependent social economy is not as clearly seen as it was in the days of our founding fathers. With the growth of interstate commerce, for example, federal "intervention" has been complete in the regulation of this commerce, and consequently state lines mean far less than in pioneer days. This blurring of the functional significance of state, county, and city boundary lines is seen also as metropolitan areas developed. The "states rights" argument against further federal participation in our national economic and social life seems less pertinent as each part of our economic and social structure depends more and more upon the health of the total structure. The informed legislator is, of course, aware of such changes in the actual functioning of the federal government. "States rights" was once a political party difference but the use of the argument now appears to be more a reflection of a fear of federal control accompanying even minimal federal contribution than any reasoning back to Constitutional provisions. A look at this danger in federal aid to education may illustrate this problem. How much is our fear justified?

Over the years the federal government has made many provisions for contributions to education in the states, and yet it is difficult to find instances where any direct control has followed participation. The Morrill Act of 1862 and the Second Morrill Act of 1890 providing subsidy to land-grant colleges, the Smith-Hughes and other acts supporting vocational education are cases in point. A recently reported study of Public Law 874 bears on this issue. The 1950 law provides funds for maintenance and operation directly to nearly 4,000 school districts in the United States that are impacted by a federal military base or a federal defense plant activity.

A study of the first five years of experience with this law was reported in 1957 in an independent study by Robert I. Sperber. Inquiry forms were sent to a sampling of the school districts and reports were received from 70 per cent of them. Between 99 and 100 per cent reported "no influence" of federal control in the administration of this act by the U. S. Commission of Education. One question posed a very direct inquiry on whether the federal government had exercised any control as the result of sending money directly to the local district. The response was an unqualified "no control" from all but one of the 500 school districts spread throughout the United States. Comments Sperber, "Never had the popular theory 'he who pays the piper calls the tune' been subjected to such close scrutiny as in the examination of this section."

Some astute Congressional leaders say quite frankly that certain disguises are used to secure voting support for bills providing federal aid to education. These may invoke the term "national defense" or the bill is presented as a temporary measure in order to protect the traditional concept of Federalism but still permit legislators to enact legislation which is in the national interest. Congressmen are men of action, responsive to public need, and will "bend the theory" to achieve results. It seems quite possible that heavy support of the National Defense Education Act of 1958 came from senators and representatives who were stressing *National Education* as much as *Defense* because they believe per se in some type of federal aid to our nation's schools.

Of course these two escape clauses of "defense" and "temporary" are used for other legislation as well — the defense system of highways, temporary provisions for urban renewal, for stream pollution control, etc. Our inconsistency shows up in another interesting way when federal attention to farm youth is hailed as being in "the old American tradition" but the same attention to city youth is viewed as "federal interference" or "creeping socialism."

There are alternative approaches to finding adequate support for so-called local services. Certainly the expanding need for public services in education, delinquency prevention, housing, etc., finds local governments hard pressed to provide adequate financial support. It seems likely that under present provisions local governments will be unable during the next decades to support these pressing social needs. Either the services will not be provided or new financial resources must be found. Since 1946 federal revenue has risen by 74 per cent (considerably less than the economy has grown) but state and local revenues have gone up by more than 300 per cent. Federal indebtedness has risen by five per cent, but state and local debt has risen 309 per cent. Clearly it is the state and local taxpayer who has already had the greatest increases levied upon him.

A variety of income sources are tapped by local governments with the share carried by the property tax lessening. State sales tax collections totaled $4⅓ billion in 1960, up 16 per cent from 1959. Such taxes yielded more than state income tax collections in 30 states. Local non-property taxes are levied in scores of communities. There is also steadily growing contribution from state and federal governments. In 1958 the federal government (via the state) and the state government distributed over $8⅓ billion to local governments, 27 per cent of their revenue from all sources. Urban, and even more the metropolitan centers, are a matter of state and national concern and will become increasingly so in the future.

*A Charge to the Counselor*

There is a fear — and a justified one — that an individual may become too dependent upon his government. There is a growing concentration of people in limited living areas, a growing interdependence of geographic areas and economic units within our country, a growing need for national cohesion because other parts of the world are so near, other peoples are "breathing down our neck." In the face of these conditions, dependence needs become strong. The counselor must have a well-developed philosophy of his own with regard to independence and its relation to cooperative living if he is to be a source of strength to students. Where does the truth lie between the extremes of selfish individualism and rampant social directiveness?

If the counselor is to be useful to both students and staff he cannot afford the luxury of remoteness from citizenship reality. Nor can he permit his own attitudes toward changes in government to go unexamined. He cannot allow 1900 perceptions of federal government to be applied to 1960 or 1970 conditions. Yet there *are* principles involved — and how apply an ancient principle with modern tools? What is it to be a citizen? Well, to be an informed citizen of community, state, nation, and world isn't easy. Of all these it is probably most difficult to know how to be a committed citizen of our nation — to be an American.

## The World Next Door

No private program and no public policy, in any section of our national life, can now escape from the compelling fact that if it is not framed with reference to the rest of the world it is framed with perfect futility.

— HENRY L. STIMSON

The thoughtful American is deeply troubled about the place of America in a world of a hundred other nations. He has always thought of America as militarily secure, both in terms of its geographical isolation and its unique industrial power. Since World War II he has been made vividly aware that these conditions are changing. He has for generations taken pride in the respect accorded America by other nations, respect for our tradition of democracy, for our origin as a nation founded upon the fought-for principles of individual rights and equal representation. He is unhappily aware that something has happened to this sense of universal respect. Some parts of the world are actively hostile to us; other parts are resentful and bitterly critical of us. This is a new experience for our American, and he has been wont to think defensively in attributing this to the propaganda of "enemies." More recently he has become uneasily aware that only part of the changed attitude can be laid at the door of totalitarian states, that some aspects of our own society need close scrutiny.

Still more recently has our thoughtful American become sensitized to the reality that America has world economic competitors of growing strength.

America is a strong nation among nations and is either respected or feared by the rest of the world. She stands for something significant but the image of just what this is has become less distinct of late. She is free of territorial ambitions, this seems abundantly clear. She stands for peace, but so all nations avow. The Rockefeller Panel Report on U. S. Foreign Policy describes the image of America in terms of a new definition of "national interest." This involves certain characteristics of the ideal America and of the American conception of the ideal world.

The first ideal defines America as "an experiment in human liberty"; as a nation with a sense of being watched "by others who have high expectations of us" but who are aware of "the deep contradictions within the American system which derive from slavery . . ."; as a nation believing deeply that "the state exists for man, not the other way around"; that government is to be "by the consent of the governed"; that all men of all nations are endowed with inalienable rights for "life, liberty, and the pursuit of happiness."

The second ideal is that of the world at peace, based on separate political units acting as a community. "Within this community there need not be and should not be uniformity; diversity of religion, culture, philosophy, social organization, expression, and ideals is to be expected. The international community thus conceived ought to include any state which does not insist on imposing its way of life on others." This community of states must develop cooperatively, assisting those that may need help, but beyond this to build institutions and arrangements for common action and development. These may first be in technical fields and by regions to meet the conditions brought about by increased populations, rising standards of living, heightened expectations, immediacy of communication, and vastly increased contact between communities and peoples.

This is a brave image, clear as a clarion call. There remains our operational acceptance of it, our filling in of the image both economically and socially.

## Rising Tide of Expectations

This phrase has been used by various writers to describe a world psychological phenomenon. Peoples throughout the world are aware of the availability to the developed nations of the comforts of life, and, quite simply, they want them too. The Stanford Research Institute, in a report for the Senate Committee on Foreign Relations, says: "The world in which we live is a world divided not merely into two camps — ours and that of the Communists — it is also a world divided into other camps, such as the traditional and the modern, the rich and the poor, the hungry and the satiated, the illiterate and the educated, the free and the oppressed. Potentially the most tremendous social force in the world of the 1960's will be the people who know they no longer have to be hungry and poor, who want education and freedom, who want bicycles, refrigerators, movies, and radios, who want to see the city, who want what science and technology have made possible in the West, and who want it now."

Economists suggest that there is urgency in this situation. These peoples are industrializing and increasing their food production. Neither is being done rapidly enough even to keep abreast of the increase in population let alone meet the increased expectations for more food and more amenities. The gap between the industrially developed nations and those in the first stages of industrialization will increase in the next 10 years unless strenuous efforts are made by us to lessen it. We cannot, within the foreseeable future, close the gap.

Population control would help materially but this will require a special kind of assistance. America must contribute financially but she must also supply people and knowledge. We must provide technical assistance of various kinds including group psychologists and specialists in social communication. Quite specifically, population control and increased food production both depend more heavily upon educating people to accept what we now know technically than upon improved technical procedures. Our own survival as one nation in a constantly shrinking world requires that we motivate the larger and more undernourished populations to move toward a decrease in births and an increase in food production, as well as to develop their own industrial world.

## What Is the American's Attitude?

Much of what has been written here sounds very selfish indeed. We aid them so they won't affiliate with our enemy — so that we can get the benefit of their trade rather than the totalitarian block. Perhaps we need to aid them from a *primary* motive of human concern for them. There is much that we might try to do for them that will backfire upon us unless our motive is one of love rather than self-interest. No one likes gifts unless self-respect is retained as the gift is accepted. It is possible that we need to know much more *about* other peoples before we know enough to help them.

There is something very inconsistent too about our emphasis upon the equality of all men coupled with our frequent use of the terms "underprivileged," "underdeveloped," or "backward" people. These descriptive terms imply an evaluation of others but always from where we are — and we see ourselves as at the apex. Other cultures are "underprivileged" because they do not have the privileges of life that we have — they are "backward" of us. In some matters of human existence — sufficient food, control of disease, freedom of speech, opportunities for learning, freedom from coercion — we may be right in assuming that they should be possessed by all men. On the other hand, bathtubs, air conditioning, and automobiles are privileges for us, but other nations have advanced cultures without them. "Cleanliness is next to godliness" has its health implications but only in some parts of the world is it a broadly cultural value. Automobiles get us places faster but we may see less along the way than do those who walk.

There is also frequent use of the phrase "uncommitted nations" in a bland assumption that this means uncommitted to either of two ways of life and forms of government, but there are many ways. A Cambridge professor, D. W. Brogan, in *Adventures of the Mind* speaks of the amazement of Americans that the fall of empires and the rise of nationalism does not always mean nationalism in the American manner. Nationalism may actually be more suppressive than colonialism. It is time for the empires to go but the many new nationalisms that arise may be offensive to the American if he views them only from the vantage point of the American revolution and the nationalism it produced. Many nations will be seen running before they can walk, many demanding steel mills when they have more need for wells and better seed. And they may move in many ways, yet the awkward nationalist world is that in which we must all now live. The Urdu language has six words for "command" but no word for "independence."

### The Counselor's Responsibility in This Shrinking, Jostling World

The American school counselor must become aware of the developing peoples of the world if he is to keep in touch with his students. Through the medium of worldwide television the sights and sounds of streets in New Delhi or Buenos Aires may be more common to every living room than the streets of an American city a thousand miles away. This American counselor cannot afford to be culturally "just" American for he is becoming a world citizen. He must learn to appreciate the 5,000-year-old history of the Arabs and their pride in it, the contribution of contemplation made by India, the long history of art in China. Some of the greatest natural scenic wonders on our planet are in South America and Africa; the Prado in Spain is one of the two or three top art museums in the world.

During the next decade or two, increasing numbers of young Americans will work in other parts of the globe as natural and social scientists, technicians, and businessmen. Unlike Americans (or Englishmen or Hollanders) in the past, they dare not carry their culture with them but must be willing to learn from the new culture and become a part of it. Citizens in many of the newer nations of the world are "touchy" about Americans. They sense in us an arrogance which may or may not be present, a condescending attitude of one who comes from bountiful

America. If our young worker is to "help" that country it will be in terms of *its* values and needs, not his own. This may be a new nation but not a new culture. He must be willing to learn as well as to contribute. Nor must he expect gratitude for few students are grateful to teachers no matter how much they learn.

*The Art of Overseasmanship* estimates that from 1956 to 1959 the number of Americans working abroad increased almost 25 per cent. With such an acceleration facing us it is urgent to examine the qualities needed for effective overseas performance. Experience thus far suggests these: (1) technical skill; (2) belief in the mission, *i.e.*, dedication to his work regardless of geography; (3) cultural empathy — the desire to study and the skill to perceive the inner logic and coherence of the other person's way of thinking; (4) a sensitivity to how one's self affects the power structure around him; and (5) organizational ability and an understanding of complicated field relationships. Some of the "backward" nations of the world will move more rapidly than we have because they can pick up all of the innovations that have been developed in other cultures. They will not have to go through each period of our industrial revolution to reach the point where they can have Ramblers or Renaults. Nigeria is to have, within a year or two, aptitude tests that are adapted completely to their culture and an electronic computer system for the maintenance of their school records that will be superior to that in most of our American cities. Our young American overseas must conceive of himself as in a "developing" nation, not an "underdeveloped" one.

Both counselor and student must see the rapid shrinking of the world, the closeness to us of other peoples. Many have cultures of greater antiquity than ours by one or several millenia. Many are warmer-hearted and more friendly than we as people even though their governments may be in an uncertain relation to our own.

It is important that the present conflict does not cause us to wear blinders and see only the Communist world and our own. There are the other countries of our own Western Hemisphere, so close to us in history and values, with all but three countries of this hemisphere using another language than our own. There is the great free world of Western Europe, from whence came so many of our ancestors. There is the rim of Asia from Japan to India via the Philippines and Australia with its ancient cultures and its modern ones. There is the Middle East with so much to teach us and so much to learn. There is the great continent of Africa with its fiercely proud new awareness of itself. This world is exciting for a young person to contemplate — and so close.

# CHAPTER 3 — CONTENTS

# Changing Ideas About Human Behavior

THE COUNSELOR who studied psychology a decade ago and then busied himself helping young people, to the neglect of professional journals and new ideas, has a conceptual revolution to catch up with. "Things aren't as they used to be" fully as much in the science of behavior as in our changing culture. Nor can the counselor depend upon paperbacks and popular treatments of psychology. What is now known by the behavioral scientist is considerably in advance of popular psychology. Research has moved on apace, following new strategies and speeded incredibly by the advent of electronic computers.

Today test results are assumed to provide only a fraction of the picture of a man even if the tests are carefully conceived and are standardized by modern methods. Occupational appraisal is far more than aptitudes. Motivation cannot be determined with assurance from what a person says about himself. For a counselor to attempt to do his job with a few aptitude tests and some informational booklets would be analogous to a surgeon's operating with only a scalpel. To understand a student through the use of a general intelligence test and a school record would be like trying to understand the United States through the use of a map of the East Coast.

Counseling is at once a profession and a human art. Like all true professions, it is rooted in and draws sustenance from an established body of knowledge. Just as medicine is founded upon such basic sciences as biochemistry, anatomy, and physiology so counseling is founded upon its appropriate disciplines of the social sciences and the behavioral sciences. In the preceding chapter we have examined in some detail the social forces that the counselor and his client must reckon with as they try together to make sensible projections of life plans. This has received heavy emphasis in this report not because it is of greater importance than the study of the individual but because it has been neglected or treated too lightly in earlier conceptions of the counselor's task. None of this is to suggest, however, that the counselor is to neglect his first and perhaps greater love, the study of the individual. What has been happening here is fully as dramatic as are the changes in our culture. "The frontier behind the forehead" has been the scene of much activity, and new understandings of what happens there are as exciting as they are useful.

## The Nature of Human Abilities

Note in the first place that the plural term is used. There is a constellation of abilities with which the counselor must be concerned and, of these, general (or abstract or verbal) intelligence is only one. Far too often in the past the counselor has offered little more than the implications of an intelligence test score and perhaps some measurement of his pattern of interests to the student who, for example, is considering the all-important question of his educational future. Yet we know that an ever-so-good general aptitude test score accounts for only about 35 per cent of the factors related to academic success in college. We know also that an interest test score when carefully interpreted provides some cues on vocational or social motivation but not much on scholastic motivation.

Today several long-range research programs promise to provide us with more adequate information on abilities. One will serve as an example. J. P. Guilford has worked for years on what is called a "factor analysis" of human abilities. He finds five kinds of intellectual processes which he classifies as factors of understanding (cognition), memory, orderly thinking (convergent thinking), creativity (divergent thinking), and comparison (evaluation). When these operations are applied to content areas, we may speak roughly of four kinds of intelligence.

The first is "concrete" intelligence for those who work most effectively with concrete things and their properties (mechanics, operators of machines, some aspects of an engineer's work, artists, and musicians).

We have, secondly, two kinds of "abstract" intelligence. Symbolic intelligence is important in the study of languages and mathematics, whereas semantic intelligence is important for understanding in terms of verbal concepts. The latter becomes important in all courses where the learning of facts and ideas is essential.

The fourth is "social" intelligence which contributes to understanding the behavior of others and of ourselves. This is largely nonverbal in character but subdivides into as many as 30 abilities, some having to do with productive thinking about behavior and some with the evaluation of behavior. Social intelligence is all important to such people as as teachers, law officials, social workers, therapists, politicians, statesmen, and leaders of various kinds. Guilford writes, "With about fifty factors already known, we may say there are at least fifty ways of being intelligent" which theoretically involve as many as 120 distinct abilities.

## The Recognition of Talent

To discharge his responsibilities to society and to the individual, the counselor needs a more inclusive and a more differentiating conception of human abilities than has frequently been adopted in our schools. We have tended to define ability in terms of performance on an intelligence test. The availability of a reasonably accurate instrument for measuring one kind of competence has led us to neglect other abilities. Talent should be defined as high level performance in any valuable line of human activity. This goes far beyond the verbal and numerical, to the appreciative, the aesthetic, the social, the mechanical.

It is relatively easy to see that our definition of ability should include talent in art, music, literary expression, human relationships, leadership, and so on through a long list of socially and individually valued competencies. What is less easy to do is to *recognize and accept* these varied talents. Sometimes the adult doesn't have the appropriate language to get into communication with a student about a particular talent, sometimes the talented person is too different to be comfortable to have around. Getzells and Jackson studied a group of bright adolescents who were divided into two groups: those with high IQ scores and lower scores on several measures of creativity and those with high creativity scores and lower (but still high) scores on measures of intelligence. Both groups did equally well in school but the high creatives had more varied occupational interests and less conventional conceptions of what would constitute success in life. In school, the low creative but bright student wanted to have personal qualities which were quite in harmony with teacher values while the high creative student wanted qualities often at odds with teacher preferences.

In an exhaustive study of men graduate students at the University of California, MacKinnon found that two variables contributed to effective personality functioning: (a) emotional stability or personal soundness, (b) originality or creativity of thought and action. The background of the emotionally stable, as compared with those less stable, was characterized by an unusually healthy childhood, integrity and stability in the home including a father seen as a respected, successful individual and a mother who was affectionate and both of whom gave their close attention to the children. Characteristic also of these men was the presence of other children in the home with whom they had generally friendly relations, experience in sports and competitive activities, a history of normal and stable sexual development. All of this is "in the groove" of normal expectations.

When the highly original or creative student was examined a different story was told. The home background was often not healthy, with much friction and many emotional obstacles to be overcome. It was almost as though the creative (those who lasted to graduate school!) had sharpened their capacity for thinking differently by having had obstacles to overcome. Certainly they were, in comparison with the less creative, more spontaneous and aggressive, had a higher level of energy in their work, appreciated the aesthetic as well as the intellectually theoretical, scored high in feminine characteristics, were skeptical and somewhat rebellious in school.

Such studies as these should make the counselor more appreciative of the complexity of "talent" and more aware of the skill it takes to understand and deal with it. Remarkable people may come from most unlikely backgrounds, be overwhelmingly complex and inconsistent, be difficult to love. Yet these are the ones for whom counselors, of all school people, must feel the greatest responsibility.

We see more clearly today than formerly that the goals and strategies of the counselor are shaped by concern for both the individual and society. The individual draws heavily upon society and he can be expected to contribute in turn to its strength and character. But the opposite is true also — society owes it to the individual to allow him to contribute in his own unique way. The relationship between society and the individual is a reciprocal one with the counselor serving as mediator. Dael Wolfle argues that in part because society *needs* a diversity of talents, society should maximize diversity both among individuals and within a given individual. The counselor is an agent of society not only when he helps students to understand society's needs for a wide range of talents but also when he provides encouragement and protection for the individual who develops uniquely. The many-talented, well-balanced person is easy to encourage but should we always try for the "rounded" individual? If we do we may cheat society for there is need for some people "who may be called uneven or one-sided but in whom at least one side has developed to the point of real superiority."

## Four Major Influences in Psychological Thinking

Before looking at other areas of research it will be helpful to understand four current and influential ways of thinking about people.

Counselors and all who deal professionally with human behavior have been strongly influenced over the past 30 - 40 years, whether they recognized it or not, by two major movements: *psychoanalytic concepts* of the origin and nature of behavior and the brutally simple precepts of *behaviorism*. These have completely divergent approaches to the understanding of behavior, one stressing the total behavior pattern as seen from within, the other focusing upon separate elements of behavior as seen from without. Still very powerful, perhaps the most powerful, influences in psychological thinking are the modern movements of *a neo-psychoanalysis* with its social determinants of behavior as well as its biological, and *a neo-behaviorism* which uses scientific method to study not only simple habit formation but motivation, individual purpose, and value determination.

A third and more recent movement is an outgrowth of modern psychoanalytic thought. This is a study of the development of a person's self as it is influenced by how he sees himself and how he responds to the ways that others see him. This is known as "ego-psychology" or *"self theory."*

A fourth movement has different roots entirely. It is a study of self also but merges the study of behavior as such with inquiry into its philosophical meanings. *Existentialism* has its roots in philosophy and theology and is a strange bedfellow for behaviorism. Nevertheless the movement of our inquiry from observable behavior and the meaning of such behavior to the individual is logically followed by a concern for the meaning of existence itself.

Counselors who want to catch up with the times on these four areas will find such books as the following both clear and stimulating: K. Horney, *The Neurotic Personality of our Time* (1937); E. H. Erikson, *Childhood and Society* (1950); A. Wheelis, *The Quest for Identity*, (1958); G. W. Allport, *Becoming* (1955); the first essay in Rollo May, *et al.*, *Existence* (1959); Carl Rogers, *On Becoming a Person* (1961).

## New Concepts in Learning

Since counseling is designed to be a learning process, the counselor must know something of the research which deals with the psychological processes in learning. As in the discussion of human abilities, one major research approach must serve to illustrate, and in this case it will be the work of B. F. Skinner. Few developments in psychology have stirred up as much research as have his studies of "operant conditioning." In spite of its formidable label, the principles involved are easy to grasp. To insure behavior changes taking place in the desired direction, the desired behavior is first described and a suitable reinforcement or reward established. When the individual acts in a way approximating the desired behavior, a reward is forthcoming immediately, thus increasing the possibility of the response being repeated. Undesired responses go unrewarded. As the desired behavior is more closely approximated, rewards occur more frequently until the subject is regularly emitting the specific response desired by the experimenter. The spacing of rewards is also manipulated, for this controls the continuation of the desired behavior. Thus the learner is led along much as a boy leads a cat down a path by dragging a piece of string.

Let us look at some experimentally demonstrated effects of this principle of learning, selecting those having particular pertinence to the work of the counselor. Greenspoon asked subjects to name as many nouns as they could. When a subject named a plural noun, the experimenter said, "uh-huh," (thus administering a verbal reinforcement). As a result the subjects gradually produced more and more plural nouns, although they were not aware that the experimenter was shaping their behavior. In another experiment, students were interviewed by telephone concerning their opinions of the general education program of their college. With one group, the interviewer quietly said "good" after each favorable statement. With another group, the interviewer said "good" after each *un*favorable statement. The first group expressed increasingly favorable opinions and the second group increasingly unfavorable opinions of the general education program, and neither group was aware that its opinions were being influenced by the interviewer.

A third experiment demonstrates that a subject's references to the self can be increased or diminished at the will of the experimenter. The experimenter engaged a subject in an interview on a broad topic. During the first 10 minutes, the experimenter remained quiet if the subject got quiet; the second 10 minute period, he responded to statements having "I," "me," "my," "mine," "myself," etc., in them; in the final period, he reverted to his noncommittal responses. Curves representing frequency of self-references were drawn. Few self-references were expressed in the first period; there was a sharp rise in the second period; and, in the final period, the curve showed a gradual extinction of the response, accompanied for some subjects by obvious annoyance. Finally, to mention only one more of many similar studies, schizophrenic patients were led to talk about formerly avoided emotional topics by a therapist who reinforced emotionally laden statements and let pass unrewarded statements that were of a more neutral character.

Clearly, what a person says is shaped by what is said to him, and in accordance with lawful patterns. Other studies have proved the effectiveness of "body language" in an interview. A counselor can reinforce as surely as with words by using body movements of leaning forward, facial expressions of interest, direction and intensity of gaze, etc.

58

Experienced counselors have long known the danger of projecting one's biases into the thinking of a client, but these have been assumed to be gross effects rather readily guarded against. Now the counselor cannot be sure of his neutrality. In the studies of verbal reinforcement cited above, we see the mechanisms of such projections laid bare; we see the subtle power of seemingly innocuous words; we see the danger of quite unconsciously leading a client down sinuous paths of obscure intent. More important, we see a powerful technique which is almost frightening in its effectiveness.

A cautionary note is in order. The counselor is a person too, and his behavior can be shaped by a client. In one study arrangements were made for advanced graduate students to give an intelligence test to some undergraduates, who were in collaboration with the experimenter. Half of the undergraduates were instructed to act warm and interested; the other half cool and bored. Both groups gave the same memorized responses to the test. The examiners gave more help to the "warm" students and found them to be more intelligent! Counselors could well afford to read B. F. Skinner, *Science and Human Behavior*, 1953.

A second caution has been hinted at earlier. Does a counselor *want* to accept the responsibility of utilizing this approach? Does he want to "play God"? Skinner says he can't help it, he will anyway. Rogers does not agree. Perhaps the counselor should read Rogers in conjunction with Skinner (*On Becoming a Person* or any of his earlier books).

The larger context within which the learning process takes place is succinctly described by Jerome S. Bruner in *The Process of Education* (1960). This small book presents a distinctly different approach to such topics as the structure of knowledge in the intellective process, readiness for learning, intuitive and analytic thinking, and motivations for learning. Research on these cognitive processes is now being conducted by Bruner and Miller at Harvard's new Center for Cognitive Studies. Teachers and counselors will find the Bruner book rewarding.

## Personality Appraisal and Vocational Choice

In order to help a student a counselor must know how to help him understand himself. Vocational choice is seen as a process, not an event, with many choices made over a lifetime. The validity of the choices made will increase as the individual increases in clarity of self-understanding as well as in understanding better the world of work. The present century has seen much stress upon more accurate measurement of specific psychological characteristics. Currently, attention is being given to another emphasis, the study of the developmental pattern of a person's life, the stages by which he arrived at where he is now. One approach provides a cross-section picture of the person, the other a vertical or longitudinal description. Either approach is incomplete without the other.

Psychological descriptions of the cross-sectional variety are now seen to be enormously more complicated than they were once thought to be. Each facet of the personality is related dynamically to every other facet and its function is affected by the functioning of the other parts of the whole. Tests containing several known factors, a test battery of several separate tests, a profile of interrelated scores — these are the pattern of the day. Tests that are validated against immediate criteria — success in training or with an entry job — may not predict longer range or more complex criteria — a job two steps up the ladder and five years later. It is like saying that a suit that fits a boy of 14 is not likely to fit him when he is 18.

Nowhere can we get a better sense of the new dimensions of the problem of appraisal than in the bold and formidable Project TALENT of John C. Flanagan. This project, described further in Chapter 5, in the spring of 1960 secured 58 test and inventory scores on each of 440,000 high school students. These measures of ability, aptitude, achievement, and background factors provide the largest and most complete reservoir of information about secondary school students ever collected in this country. The frequencies and the intercorrelations of the measures on students will provide invaluable information about aptitudes and the school and community settings in which these aptitudes exist. The influence on vocational counseling should be marked.

But cross-section measurement is not accepted by all as the most important. Predictive appraisal based upon tests seems quite inadequate to some research workers. (It does even to Flanagan who will study test scores against home backgrounds.) A "true natural history" science of behavior would depend upon observations of behavior in the natural settings of life. Less accurate but more meaningful would be intelligence appraised by how a person behaved in normal, not artificial settings — in his home, the playground, on the job — rather than with a carefully standardized test. Most usefully the cross sectional would be supplemented by the developmental.

In keeping with this second emphasis is an energetic school of thought dealing with new concepts of vocational development. In the long-range research projects that have been launched in America, notably by Super at Teachers College, Columbia, and by Tiedeman at Harvard, as well as in France and Japan, attention is paid to the totality of the "career pattern" of the individual. This includes his pattern of choices made while in school. Cross-section measurements may be made but always as part of the study of the developmental pattern. The vocational development emphasis makes possible a closer tie of vocational choice and adjustment to developmental psychology and environmental conditioning than was possible in previous approaches. Most significantly there is an emphasis upon sequential and lawful (hence predictable, it is hoped) stages of vocational choice and realization through the life span. It is too early to say what these efforts will yield in terms of a sturdy theory of vocational choice and development, yet it is clear that they will probably require the counselor to recast his thinking about the individual into new forms. Good reading for the counselor would be Donald E. Super's *The Psychology of Careers* (1956) and Leo Goldman's *Using Tests in Counseling* (1961).

## New Conceptions of Motivation

In many respects the core problem for the individual student, for the counselor, and for the school, is how the student may channel his energy into activity that is both personally satisfying and socially acceptable. This is the problem of motivation. Few areas of psychology in the past decade have seen such lively and productive inquiry.

Inquiries about motivation have ranged from studies of brain functioning to studies of life goals. Only two or three illustrations can be given here. One basic study showed how dependent man is upon input from his environment to keep himself oriented and appropriately in touch with his world. In a series of experiments at McGill University by Bexton and his colleagues, students were paid generously to undergo a period of sensory deprivation. They were put in a small room with a cot. All sound was masked, goggles eliminated form vision, and gloves and elbow cuffs reduced tactile stimulation. The students at first thought this would be an easy way to get rich quick, but they soon changed their minds. After a couple of days of sensory starvation, washing restaurant dishes at low pay seemed very attractive indeed. During the experiments subjects were allowed to listen to recorded nursery rhymes, old stock market reports, and a temperance lecture, and they demanded encore after encore. Many subjects began to hallucinate, to see animals marching across the ceiling, and to feel themselves separated from their bodies. After the period of sensory deprivation, many subjects required a considerable period to re-establish contact with their worlds. The removal of sensory input is like throwing a machine out of gear; the motor, deprived of necessary friction, runs away.

One of the most provocative formulations of the problem of human motivation is provided by Maslow's theory of a hierarchy of motives, which must be satisfied from lower to higher levels for a person to express his most human attributes. This structure from low to high is as follows: (1) physiological needs — for food, water, etc.; (2) safety needs — for a reasonably safe, orderly, and predictable world; (3) belongingness and love needs — for affectionate relationships with people; (4) esteem needs — for achievement, adequacy, mastery, competence, and independence; (5) the need for self-realization — a sense of living what you actually are; (6) cognitive needs — for knowing and understanding; and (7) aesthetic needs — for beauty and harmony. Man's most essential characteristics, his capacity for creation, for compassion, for aesthetic response, involve what Maslow terms "growth motivation" and come into play only when lower order needs are satisfied.

The counselor today, as he scans the literature on the nature of the individual, will find a new emphasis on man as *problem seeker* as well as *problem solver*. Older psychologies focused largely on escape from hunger, thirst, pain, or sexual tension, as the mainsprings of human behavior. Freudian psychology built its theory of motivation on sexual and aggressive instincts. Both of these formulations seem to miss one of the most distinctive characteristics of man — his need to explore, to reach out, to find new meanings in experience. Man searches for the joy of searching, no matter how upsetting is the process. Man does indeed seek equilibrium but he also seems to get his greatest joy from upsetting things. He seems most vigorously human when he deliberately precipitates himself into just-manageable difficulties, then works to restore order. The counselor who accepts this concept of human nature will have a new dynamic to rely upon.

## Broad Frontiers for the Counselor

Although both have been mentioned earlier, there seems good reason to scrutinize both values and self-identification in this chapter on psychological frontiers.

### Student and Counselor Values

It has become increasingly clear that the counselor cannot and does not remain neutral in the face of the student's value conflicts. Even the counselors who believe most strongly in letting the student work out his own solutions have firm values of their own and cannot help communicating them. They communicate their values in what they do and don't do even if they never mention their beliefs verbally. Furthermore, we expect more and more of the counselor with reference to the needs of society. Just to accept the need for the full development of abilities in the interest of a stronger nation as well as the interest of the individual is a manifest expression of a social value. Because the counselor cannot escape dealing with values and expressing values in his own behavior, he must be clear about the nature of his own values and how they influence his relationships with other people.

A second developing conviction about values is that they are now seen by some psychologists as the central difficulty for many troubled people. Fifty years ago values were clearly defined, and acute maladjustment seemed to result from a willful violation of them. Psychological treatment consisted primarily of freeing the individual from an overwhelming sense of guilt over his transgression against his parents and other representatives of society. But today the picture seems almost the reverse of what it was. The maladjusted person feels himself more lost than guilty. Social expectations have become more diverse, less well defined, less insistent. The social processes of inculcating strong values are less effective today, in part because family and community are less cohesive.

As a consequence the individual feels a lack of purpose and direction. He feels estranged from others and even from himself; he feels worthless and unsure of his identity. He must discover character in himself for himself. Values strongly felt are the foundation upon which he can build an increasingly satisfying personal existence. Thus, clarifying values and perhaps acquiring new values becomes a major task for the individual in counseling, as in education generally.

The counselor may be understandably reluctant to assume that his values are "right" for other persons. But he must at least deal with those inconsistencies and contradictions in values which stand in the way of the student's efforts to cope with problems.

## The Achievement of Identity

As stated in Chapter 1, adolescence is a period of intense involvement with the problem of achieving identity. For the individual it is a period of almost explosive becoming. It is a period of close to full physical development, of intense sexuality both specific and diffuse, of intelligence approaching full power, of knowledge that cumulates with increasing speed and relevance, of freedom to move around both physically and intellectually. For society, adolescence is a period of preparation for adult responsibility in marriage, in work, and in community affairs. But observers of the interaction between the individual adolescent and society see many disjunctions. The counselor's business is appropriately centered at these points of disjunction and of too easy resolution. He needs all the data, all the insights he can get if he is to work effectively with individuals.

It should not be surprising that the adolescent will have difficulty in establishing identity in a mass, industrialized society in which anonymity is encouraged and the absurd is magnified. It is a hard fact that the adolescent cannot participate in the productive enterprises of adults; he is kept off the labor market and denied the maturing experiences of an early apprenticeship or other responsibility for making society work. His sense of uselessness to society is high. Indeed, some maintain that the chief function of the adolescent in our society is to consume goods. In such a society there is nothing for the adolescent to pit himself against in an effort to find out who he is.

In England, the "Outward Bound Schools" attempt to remedy this defect. Industries send their shipping clerks and accountants and customers' men to rugged camps where they pit themselves against rock cliffs and the open sea in small boats to discover individuality and autonomy as well as responsible group membership. The forestry camp movement in the United States has a similar intent, in part.

There is some evidence that girls in our society have adult models more available to them than do boys whose task of achieving identity is made difficult by the absence or elusiveness of adequate men in their teen-age world. Sociologist Martin B. Loeb points out that girls in the home have many opportunities to identify with the mother and to develop some sense of the woman's role as far as homemaking is concerned. On the contrary, boys see little of the father in his masculine role in the world of work and have little opportunity to identify with adult males in general. Men in his life do things *for* him — teachers, playground directors, etc. — but few things *with* him in adult activities. Fathers are encouraged to participate with their sons but increasingly at the son's level, not the father's. Risk and a chance to prove himself are minimized. The boy is kept off of the labor market even more than girls who can at least baby-sit. Vocational counseling itself is too remote from try-out experiences and from any chance for the young people to secure a sense of work achievement. The protection from risk-taking in a vocational role or an adult role contributes to the boy's testing himself in antisocial ways where the standards of achievement are the immature standards of his peers.

There are, however, other hard facts that are encouraging, and there are more optimistic appraisals of the current situation with respect to the opportunity for individual development.

Studies of bright high school students find a number of young people who are already highly autonomous, creative, and committed to inquiry. There is much upward mobility; more and more young people identified as gifted come from lower socio-economic groups. Opportunities for learning, once limited to a favored few in society, are now available to many, not only through schools but also through inexpensive books, incredibly produced magazines, television, and rapid travel. Community theaters flourish. Paperbacks, and good ones, sell in huge quantities. People paint and listen to serious music and lay out cash to support orchestras. They run to the top of the best seller lists books that tell them with precious scorn and erudition how illiterate they are.

All in all, there is justification for a measured optimism with respect to the future of the individual in our society. The counselor needs to be a realist with regard to both the assets and liabilities of growing up in our culture.

# CHAPTER 4—CONTENTS

# *Changing Schools and the Counselor*

THE RIGHT to criticize is part of our American heritage. We may criticize anything and anyone — and openly. The right to open dissent is a well-defended value of our society. Schools are subject to much criticism, for education is the most encompassing single activity of our national life. If one considers parents to be as directly concerned with school as their children then we could add approximately 21 million parents to the 1960–1961 figure of 48,650,000 students, the over 2 million teachers and other staff, the 200,000 board members. This total of 72 million people means that two out of every five people in America are directly involved in education, and they have a right to be concerned about what happens in schools.

The school counselor should be deeply concerned about the criticisms of the social institution in which he works — not apprehensive but *concerned* and *informed* about the nature of the criticisms. For the students he deals with are influenced by the parents who voice these criticisms. The attitude about school that the student brings with him is likely to color his present motivation and his plans for further education. The student may expect too much or too little of the school experience, he may be influenced positively or negatively about further education. His motivation for school achievement is a concern of the counselor as well as the teacher. Often the student's perception of himself is unrealistic because he is unrealistic in his expectations of the school.

Much of the criticism of American schools has come from people who are deeply concerned but not always knowledgeable about schools. All too frequently the criticism has substance, but no solution is offered or the solution suggested is too uncompromising. What is proposed often would strengthen one educational objective while denying other educational functions which are equally worthy. The critic all too often wears blinders so that he sees only *his* goal for education. He may also be astigmatic or nearsighted so that his view of the schools or colleges is a distorted one. He may have attended private schools and colleges and wants all education, public and private, to conform to the image of his own school experience. He may be a scientist who sees the science need so great that he would have prospective scientists developed above all others.

67

The critic may have secured his own education in another country and, in his zeal, wants American schools patterned after the system of his home country. He compares education in America with education in the country of his European origin without realizing that a direct comparison of schools in two cultures is unfeasible — it is a comparison of apples and pears, each with its own flavor and its own growing season. This critic is likely also to be unaware that the American educational venture is the boldest and most daring of all American ventures, comparable to our industrial development and our freedom of public speech. Indeed, both of these would have been impossible in our country had it not been for our emphasis upon education for all to the highest degree possible for each person.

## Professional Proposals for Change

Not all criticism and proposals for the future have come from lay educators. The professional educator is likely to be sensitive to the need for change, for constant change. Most of the changes made over the years are the result of professional proposals and of dogged persistence in seeing that they were put into action. Just how much the professional has acted upon the initiative of his own critical awareness and how much in response to the demands of the public is difficult to determine. Generally speaking, however, the educational innovator has met with public resistance. Perhaps in no other societal activity is there so much of a tendency for parents and employers to want schools "as they were in my days," to put the brakes on change. Fighting for new ideas is, unfortunately, characteristic only of those who "stand tall" in the profession. Too many of the others submit weakly to public pressure for no change or carry into their teaching and administration only the perpetuation of their own educational experience.

It is literally impossible to condense the professional proposals made for the schools of the future. There are too many. The proposals of the American Association of School Administrators for a new type of year-round school calendar is one example. So is J. Lloyd Trump's *Image of the Future* and *New Directions to Quality Education* proposals from the National Association of Secondary School Principals, and the concern of the Association for Supervision and Curriculum Development ("School of the Future — 1985," *Educational Leadership*, May, 1960). Many leaders of public thought have made proposals showing much understanding of American education and containing ideas which can be directly acted upon by professional educators — John W. Gardner (*Pursuit of Excellence*; "National Goals in Education," chapter 3 of *Goals for Americans*; his 1961 book,

*Excellence*), James B. Conant (*The American High School Today*, and *A Memorandum to School Boards: Education in the Junior High School Years*), anthropologist Margaret Mead, sociologist David Riesman, writer John Hersey, etc. One striking venture initiated in 1960 was the subsidy by the Fund for the Advancement of Education of a monthly "Education Supplement" of the *Saturday Review*.

Counselors, and others, must understand that the changes proposed will be put into operation all too slowly. Social lag is very strong in our schools, and for this the layman and the professional must share the blame. The long-range problem in our schools is not increased numbers of students but *meeting the varying needs of students in terms of cultural and economic conditions of 1965 or 1970 rather than those of 1950.* Schools are not innovative enough, do not spend enough on research that would provide a sound basis for change.

Changes are being made, however, changes that the counselor must understand — changes of purpose, of organization, of procedure. Out of the many changes taking place at the beginning of the 1960's and changes that seem likely to be made in the near future, only a few will be described. These are changes which appear to reflect the social and psychological projections described in Chapters 2 and 3 and those which are thought to affect the counseling function. Sometimes the change is in the form of an emerging issue which must be faced by the counselor. The balance of this chapter will focus upon:

1. Changes in emphasis upon kinds of students and the relative importance of each to the counselor.

2. Changing purposes of education from which the counselor must choose.

3. Changes in school organization and procedures which will affect the counselor's work both directly and indirectly.

4. The increasing complexity of the transition of students from one school level to the next.

## Which Students Need the Counselor Most?

This is a rhetorical question if it suggests an assumption that some students are more important than others — *all* students are important to the counselor. Worth or need is not determined by a category label. The counselor faces a real problem of choice, however, for time demands and the arguments of those who champion different segments of the school population will require him to weigh the varying needs of at least three broad classes of students.

The academically talented are receiving a great deal of attention. This is as it should be, for failure in the past to identify students in this category and to motivate them to appropriate intellectual achievement has cost both those students and society a high price. The cost to society has been the greater perhaps, when its long-range survival needs are considered. Certainly society's loss has aroused more concern than has the loss to the individual student. We are a bit frightened not only by the advances of the totalitarian nations but by the substantial technological and social developments in such areas as Western Europe, England, Russia, and Japan. In observing both our ideological friends and enemies it behooves our society to marshal all available brain power if our leadership is not to be lost or neutralized.

The talents needed are more than the academic. They are the artistic and the mechanical as well — those with talents in human relations, in administration, and in statesmanship. In the Quincy Youth Development Study, the authors concluded that if they had added *to* the top 10 per cent of the children in general intellectual ability, the top 10 per cent in *other kinds of talent* — music, dramatic ability, creative writing, leadership, drawing ability, mechanical ability — they would have increased their 10 per cent to between 20 and 25 per cent of the total child population. Kenneth Little's study in the state of Wisconsin asked teachers to identify any of their students who were especially gifted in any field. About 20 per cent of the students so identified had not ranked in the upper quarter of their graduating class in either scholastic achievement or general mental ability. Adding other types of ability, even on an observation basis, will contribute to each school's consideration of a much larger pool of talent.

More than academic talent as such is at stake, for the creative and the innovative are the real hope of any civilization. We now know what we did not know a few years ago — that the creative person is not synonymous with the academically able. To be sure, a person to be intellectually or artistically creative must have a substantial floor of general intellectual ability, but the characteristics of the creative person are different from this point on. A student can be very intelligent and not very creative. He can be only somewhat average in intelligence and yet be markedly creative.

Studies in process at both the University of California and the University of Minnesota suggest quite clearly that creative persons have a large aesthetic element in their make-up. They score high on the Aesthetic scale as well as the Theoretical scale of such a test as the Allport-Vernon-Lindzey *Study of Values*. They possess the interests of architects, artists, and authors on the Strong *Vocational Interest Blank*. They respond to complex tasks and have a high degree of tolerance to unstructured situations which require them to find new solutions and to persist in their task until fulfillment. They are intensely curious and do not accept conventional replies to questions without proof or evidence.

The counselor must be warmly understanding of such individuals, for too many are lost to their society. This does not mean that the counselor humors them upon every occasion. These students, too, must learn to live within societal limits and to learn that their talent, whatever it may be, does not mean license to do as they individually wish. What these students need above all else is understanding of their "difference" and appreciation of their value to society. One can conjecture that many of the high school and college students who could not now be called creative were potentially so when younger, but this was squeezed out of them by the inability of adults and their peers to accept the differences which they exhibited. The question is: Can elementary and high school counselors do better?

More than incidental is the fact that the talented themselves will have a richer life and more sense of fulfillment if they can be helped to discover and to make good use of themselves. We talk much about society's need, seeming to forget that "these too" are people with sensitivity and psychological needs, often greater sensitivity than average and a greater sense of loneliness. The talented and the creative deserve competent assistance for their own sake, not only because they are vital to the welfare of society.

## Handicapped Children

At the other end of the spectrum are the physically and mentally handicapped children. So much has been done and so much remains to be done for those with varying degrees of visual and auditory deficiency, for the spastic and crippled, for the mentally subnormal, for the emotionally disturbed. Special schools, special classes, and special teachers are widely provided for these students together with state provisions for vocational training and placement.

A related and much larger category is the culturally handicapped student. Chapter 2 referred to McGill's report that a sizable proportion of the school population in the larger cities is culturally underprivileged and that this proportion is increasing yearly. Without special attention to their needs, these handicapped children will become as much, or more of, a social burden as the physically or mentally handicapped for whom special programs are provided. Their crippling deficiencies may not be as apparent or their disability as likely to stimulate sympathy. But their need is fully as real.

Others speak of "alienated students," members of minority groups who are not readily accepted by the larger school population. Their minority status may be either ethnic or economic in nature but, in any event, their isolation and sense of alienation is a crippling factor. It places a damper upon their intellectual and social development or, worse, breeds resentment and hostility.

Children in any of these categories are likely to drop out of school early. School "dropouts" occur for many reasons, the chief one perhaps being broadly expressed as the inability of the school to meet the needs of the students involved. For some youth, the local school program is simply inappropriate, and they might be better off out of school than in. For others, the program could be changed without damaging its value for the remainder of the school population. For still others, the school program may have much to contribute, but they have not been sufficiently aided to see the values involved. Professor Willis E. Dugan has specified that five groups of students contribute to an annual "waste of talent" in our country — school dropouts, students with uncorrected deficiencies, those who achieve at a level far below their capacities, those with unrealistic vocational goals, and those financially unable to continue in school. The dropout becomes a particularly serious problem in terms of both personal and social loss when one recalls the Department of Labor estimates that one-fourth of those entering the labor force in the period 1960–1970 will not graduate from high school. Opportunities for both self-respect and economic independence are increasingly limited for this group as each decade succeeds the last.

## The "Normals"

Most young people fall in between the extreme of the gifted and the handicapped. Essentially such subdivisions are unrealistic, since some of the academically able are handicapped by lack of intellectual challenge and by lack of belief in themselves. Likewise, some of the physically or culturally handicapped have substantial intellectual promise. Such grouping is unrealistic also because students do not fall into a category easily. Each student is a constellation of characteristics, some strong, some weak, some easily seen, some not. Broad categories which tag a student with a label are dangerous, indeed. This section "groups" students for ease of discussion, but in full awareness of the fallacy involved.

Some of those "whose gifts come in smaller packages" will be awakened into creativeness and leadership, some will drop into social oblivion. The majority will perform routine services, but during the next 40 years this group may be second in importance to none. Students of society are concerned about the development of an intellectual elite which may become the power group of our society. If our "universal" education does not fail us, the middle group can well become an adequate foil for, as well as an intelligent supporter of, the intellectual power group. It is they who are the stockholder-owners of our corporations, make up the membership of the labor unions and legislatures, conduct the drives, cast the votes.

Where one speaks of the need for awakening the brilliant and helping the handicapped, it must be kept in mind that the "average" citizen will have major responsibility for achieving both of these ends.

## The Counselor's Dilemma

Theoretically, the counselor must be a counselor to all, not to any *one* group, no matter how urgently its claim is advanced. He knows, too, that the major need of our heterogeneous school population is an adequately diverse educational program — curriculum, instruction, counseling. If the classroom and community learning opportunities are sufficient in number and variety and if the instructional leadership is adequate, the counselor's task seems clear. He is to help the student understand his characteristics and needs and to relate these to the most appropriate learning experiences — teacher and class, curriculum, community activity — and to the selection of the most appropriate educational and vocational goals.

Even under favorable conditions of student understanding and curriculum resources, however, the counselor will not have enough time in the day for all students. Even with a dedicated and enlightened teaching staff working closely with the majority of students, the counselor will have to choose between working with this student or that. He will not have time to help equally all who come his way. There are ways of conserving counselor time that will be presented later, but this question of the counselor remains: "What guidelines do I have for deciding how I can best apportion my time with students?"

In this connection a counselor may consider the following principles: (1) to work with those students whose developmental needs are greatest, who have most difficulty in achieving a sense of personal identity and achievement, rather than devoting major time to crisis situations in the lives of the relatively few; and (2) to work with those students for whom full under-

73

standing and motivation will mean the most to themselves and to society, those who will contribute most significantly to the societal welfare of their period.

The counselor must respond to individual need *and* societal need, not either one to the exclusion of the other. Societal needs will vary from period to period, with differing emphases on scientific discovery, technological execution, internal social advancement, international statesmanship, the world of beauty in art, literature, theatre, etc. All must be served to be sure, but the counselor must have some sense of the greatest potential need in the period that is ahead for the student. The counselor of *today* must look at *tomorrow* and say: "Where will be the greatest demand for brains and talent — scientific research, internal social health and advancement, or our nation's relations to other nations and cultures?" The logical reply may be that these are such interrelated needs that no choice is possible. Yet, in his day-to-day operations, the counselor will necessarily choose or will attempt a balance between them.

The counselor who utilizes these two principles must know much more than the characteristics and needs of the student. He must know his school's program and what it contributes to each child. He must know the immediate community pressures on different groupings of students as well as the expectations of the general culture with which the student will increasingly deal. He must develop a sensitivity to the societal and vocational needs of the decade ahead and discharge his obligation to the student's welfare in the light of projected social change.

## The Purposes of Education

School objectives change as society changes, more frequently following social change than leading it, but are always a concern of society. The effective *achievement* of these objectives is modified by professional knowledge — knowledge of human behavior, of the direction of the learning process, of sound administrative principles; so objectives are a general social concern but their attainment requires more than desire. When the layman assumes knowledge of means he is operating in dangerous territory. That is the professional's responsibility — the layman's is in the area of objectives.

The following paragraphs are not to be regarded as a systematic study. They consider four of the educational ends that are seen as of most significance to the school counselor in the light of changes in our society. Admittedly then, this is a highly selective process, and one which reflects the writer's personal judgment.

## Intellectual Development

The counselor will have to come to grips early with the increasing emphasis on intellectual development per se. This is a continuing area of conflict for the proponents of different schools of thought, but it is accentuated now by the nation's very apparent need for mathematicians, scientists, engineers — for intellectuals in many areas. Various moves by both public and private agencies (National Defense Education Act of 1958, Merit Scholarships, etc.) to identify and provide academic motivation and resources for the academically able college student are an expression of this concern. Critics of schools (particularly critics of public schools) have demanded that more attention be given to the academic subjects and to intellectual learning. Some, such as the Council for Basic Education, hold that the intellectual emphasis can be served through primary adherence to such basic subjects as English, science, history, mathematics, and foreign language. Some propose that this basic curriculum is for all students. The writer would not agree. The academic is actually only a *part* of the total intellective development.

Conant has a more moderate approach to the intellectual emphasis. He makes very clear that the academically advanced subjects are for those capable of profiting from them. For the academically able students he recommends as much work as possible in the "basic subjects," but for others, different programs of work are seen as more suitable. Conant goes even further to propose that the present school is *too academically oriented* for some adolescents. He believes that some adolescents are continually frustrated by the school experience and would be more productive and better social risks out of school than in. "It is worse for a boy," writes Conant, "to remain in school and become continually frustrated by his academic difficulties than to leave school and get a satisfying job." (Unfortunately, it is increasingly difficult for such a boy to find a satisfying job, or any job.)

The schools of this generation are clearly concerned with intellectual growth. It is not that they have ever discarded the assumption that intellectual growth is a major function of the school. The actual situation is that schools have: (a) received an increasing range of intellectual ability and academic motivation as the school system approaches a "universal" education for all pupils of school age; (b) found that attitudes affect intellectual learning, that social and emotional growth are inseparable parts of an individual's personality development and cannot be neglected if intellectual growth is to be attained; (c) been made responsible for the optimal development of all citizens in a democracy.

The school's primary function can be stated briefly. It is *to facilitate the intellectual development of students who vary widely in intellectual ability and who vary in the relation of the intellectual to the social and emotional dimensions of their personalities.* The counselor, then, is to be responsive to inter-individual differences in academic aptitude and intra-individual differences in each personality pattern. This task is far more complex and demanding than is suggested by the deceptively simple statement that "intellectual growth is a primary educational objective." The psychological setting of both group and individual within which the objective of intellectual growth is to be achieved is a major factor in achieving this essential social end.

Many schools cannot emphasize intellectual development to an appropriate degree until they have shed broad community functions which drain their energy and obscure their major purpose. Thirty years ago, this writer criticized the schools because they had assumed an "omnibus function" for society. In 1960, Dean John H. Fischer, at one time superintendent of schools in a large city, wrote:

> Virtually everything the schools are asked to do seems useful and important to someone. From producing state championship teams (primarily, of course, for the character development of the boys) to supporting the Community Chest and buying United States Savings Bonds (always to teach citizenship, of course, and never to increase the volume of collection), the schools are asked continually to extend the boundaries of their responsibility.

A school has often been seduced by the community into serving social functions which are not a part of its basic character. The school need not be a center for entertainment, civic development, and the support of charitable enterprises to fulfill its most legitimate function as a school. Some restraint is needed. Some community services performed by schools, such as organized recreation, job placement, and many phases of public health, can now be handled by community agencies that did not exist when the school undertook the task. But beyond this, the critical question remains, "Can the school serve broad community functions and at the same time discharge its major obligation to intellectual development?" Much depends, of course, upon the extent to which intellectual growth is seen as the more unique responsibility of the school. Intellectual development is interpreted here as much broader than "academic." One is a means to the other but is far from the only means.

This issue of intellectual development as the more central task of the school is vital to the counselor's perception of his role in the school. His resolution of the question will have a marked influence upon the image that others have of him and upon his usefulness in the school of the future. If many schools hew closer than formerly to broadly conceived intellectual effort, and it is projected that this may well happen, counselors either will be perceived as functioning close to the central stream of effort or as those who merely mop up around the edges. Counselors will need to see this primary school objective both for the academically able and for those less able. For if the talented are to be helped to set high intellectual standards for themselves, so are the less talented to be helped to set intellectual standards for themselves — standards appropriate to their capacities and opportunities.

## Vocational Choice and Preparation

The extent to which the school is responsible for vocational preparation is another issue with which the counselor must grapple. Pressures will intensify for the schools to prepare better the increasing proportion who continue their education beyond high school. This is in the interests of the able student as well as society. The academically able in elementary school who will be likely to attend and graduate from high school need little vocational preparation or even vocational counseling in the elementary school. Better that they are helped in academic and intellectual planning, with emphasis upon their vocational preparation and choice to come later. The same is true for those in high school who will surely attend college or university. They may well select a field of study that is intriguing to them and even choose a broad vocational area, but the more definitive vocational "finding" and preparation will come later. Their need is greater for intellectual stimulus and social development.

The less academically able are *also* in the school, however, and comprise a group of major social significance. They need vocational counseling, work experience, vocational preparation. They will leave school at the end of the compulsory school attendance period or will take programs in high school that may or may not lead to graduation. For these students, one cannot say "intellectual emphasis" to the exclusion of vocational planning and preparation. The future will see more high school graduates who do not enter college securing specific vocational training in business schools, technical institutes, hospital schools of nursing, etc., but such students will need vocational counseling in high school to prepare them for this step. Even with the consistent rise, year by year, in the proportion of those of college age who enter college, it is most likely that within the next decade, as an *average for all schools*, one-half or more of those in high school will not enter college. This proportion will vary widely, of course, from school to school. Currently, over three-fourths of those of college age are not in college. (The average is for the combined sexes; more girls than boys fail to enter college.) In any event, those not likely to enter represent a considerable number of high school students whose needs must be realistically interpreted.

It would seem that *the school could be charged with a multi-fold function of developing intellectual, social, and vocational competencies — perhaps in that order of importance.* Social intelligence and competencies are as important for those whose vocational preparation needs are served later in the school experience as for those who will enter into vocational life just following school. As a school objective, the development of social competencies serves both groups.

Work experience is a valuable means for developing social maturity if the school and community are so organized as to permit it. There is a curious reluctance to admit the educational values of part-time and summer work experiences. To be sure, unless the work experience is planned for its developmental value, the major outcome may be the money received. But in the minds of both parents and teachers "work (for pay)" and "school" are forever separated. Only the latter is "educational." Three of the Forums at the 1960 White House Conference on Children and Youth made recommendations for more planned work-school experiences. Even though the recommendations provided safeguards through the cooperation of school, parents, and employer, these recommendations met with opposition from the representatives of organized labor who saw only possible exploitation of the youth as an outcome. To deny the possibility of such reality experiences for all because of potential danger to a few would appear socially self-defeating. Some bridging of the gap between the "delayed value" experiences of the school where the daily contact is primarily with one's age peers, on the one hand, and the social reality of job demands and employer expectations, on the other hand, would seem desirable indeed.

Much more will be said about vocational counseling, for it is a major function of the school. The counselor cannot escape the "vocational choice and preparation" objective of the school for a sizable proportion of the elementary and a larger proportion of the high school student population. Vocational competency must be "paired" with intellectual development in our culture and neither be emphasized out of relationship to the other.

*Individuality*

Increasingly, the school must become effective in developing

78

individuality simultaneously with socialization. O. Meredith Wilson, President of the University of Minnesota, has described the obligations of a university as three-fold:

> . . . [first] to husband and cherish the wisdom of mankind. We communicate the best of the past to each new generation. In this sense, our role is a conservative one. A second of our obligations and one for which we should make no apology is to improve the vocational opportunities of the students who come to us for help. The third, and most commonly emphasized, and in many ways the most exciting of our obligations, is to serve as judge and critic, to refine ancient goods, and to discover new truth. In this role we are inevitably radical.

This three-fold objective for the university has its implications for the school counselor. It is not often that a university president openly accepts the vocational competency objective together with the classical ones of transmission of existing knowledge and the creation of new knowledge. So this statement is all the more stimulating. Likewise, it would be exciting to see public schools avowing that they are to "discover new truth" in an emphasis upon individuality.

It is the school counselor who, first of all, must be "radical" in encouraging individualism upon the part of a student while at the same time he helps the student see the need for living within present societal expectations and regulations. Here again, it is neither one nor the other, but both. Counselors and teachers in general are frequently accused of encouraging conformity, of seeing that students do only what is required. It is essential to be socialized, to learn systematically what is now known, to build a solid foundation of understanding the present. Such a goal, however, is not an end but the *means to the end* of creating the new and of being oneself. To understand the present and be dissatisfied with it enough to change it, to live as a member of society and yet to develop one's own pattern of being, *is to complete the process* of which present knowledge and socialization are but introductory steps.

It has been stated that Americans have lost their impetus toward individualism, that we have not recovered from the fears and insecurities of the Great Depression and World War II. It is said that we seek security through group emphasis and protection and deny the risks of personalism. The school counselor has been blamed for putting security before all else. Students are advised to train for certain vocations because the pay is good, rather than because such employment of one's talent and energies brings intellectual, spiritual, and emotional satisfactions. This kind of defensive counsel will never help to produce leadership.

Henry Wriston writes, "A guidance counselor who has made a fetish of security, or who has unwittingly surrendered his thinking to economic determinism, may steer a youth away from his dream of becoming a poet, an artist, a musician, or any other of thousands of things, because it offers no security, it does not pay well, there are no vacancies, it has no future."

The counselor must come to terms with this issue. Encouraging a student to develop his own individuality, to take risks in making long-range choices rather than to choose in the interests of security requires some assurance and courage on the part of the counselor.

To learn to live intelligently in the present and cooperatively within the group, on the one hand, to create the new for the future and to risk being different, on the other hand, is the counselor's responsibility. This responsibility is first for himself and then for the students he counsels. To be too well adjusted to the present is to incure the greater risk of unadjustment to the future. A counselor who is content and comfortable with what he learned in graduate school 10 years ago or who rationalizes that the nationalism of 1940 will "surely" continue is dangerous to himself and others. He can be likened to a man riding a bicycle on a crowded express highway where the minimum speed limit is 40 miles an hour. Someone is going to get hurt.

Some critics of "adjustment" as a goal would put things differently. Peter Vierick wrote ("The Unadjusted Man — Last Refuge of Civilization's Secret Fires," *Saturday Review*, November 1, 1958) that "without an ornery, unadjusted inner spark, our present drive for outward techniques is not enough to save us spiritually or militarily." Vierick proposes a new goal of "adjustment to the ages, unadjustment to the age. The meaningful moral choice is not between conforming and non-conforming, but between conforming to the ephemeral, stereotyped values of the moment and conforming to the ancient, lasting archetypal values shared by all creative cultures."

British philosopher Stephen Toulmin is concerned that scientists in becoming a profession tend to lose their adventuresome spirit. Professional men are expected to show results, yet science should not be so limited. "Fundamental scientific insights are a kind of intellectual capital. . . . They may start paying dividends quite soon, but equally they may not do so for centuries — or ever." The great scientists of the past are described by Toulmin as "men with the intellectual fidgits" who were not concerned with the usefulness of their insights.

Contemporary poet George Barker sees the poet as an enemy of society "because only the enemy within the gates can report anything like the truth. . . . For the poet, society is an institution dedicated wholeheartedly to the pursuit of its own lies. It is the moral duty of the poet to speak about these lies; it is what makes him a poet, it is also what makes him an enemy of society. . . . For all I seek to assert is the spiritual irresponsibility of a world that pays millions of dollars for a bomb and forty shillings for a poem."

The "unadjusted" artist and scholar, the adventuresome scientist with the intellectual fidgets, the poet who pillories the lies of society will be encountered in embryonic form by the school counselor. Will he be able to recognize them? Will he have the courage to allow them to be different? For the student must be helped to see that these excursions of mind and spirit probably will not "pay" — except in contributions upon which no one can set a price.

## International Culture

*Education for living with people of other cultures* as a school objective is as yet in its infancy. To say that it will become a major objective in the next decade or two may seem visionary to some people yet it is a realism that is essential for our survival. We must educate toward this objective very soon or be left at the post. Currently, however, education for cultural internationalism is largely a projection into the future. Two illustrations of specific projections follow.

Leonard S. Kenworthy describes "Education for the Community of 1985" (*Education Leadership*, May 1960) in the form of changes to be made in school emphasis and curriculum. Most of the changes recommended involve a better understanding of the peoples of the world:
"More and better education
about human relations
about all parts of the world
about the contributions of all people to the world
about the communications relationship of the United States
to the world
More and better experiences for pupils and teachers abroad
More and better teaching about the fun and beauty in the
world
A more realistic treatment of world problems."

Professor Kenworthy has gone further than a mere statement of the aims since he is respectively author and editor of two books on international understanding through the curriculum of elementary schools and the curriculum of secondary schools.

From a different realm of thought comes a profound treatment of the world future by F. S. C. Northrup (*Philosophical*

*Anthropology and Practical Politics*) in which the understanding of other peoples is seen as the only escape from a totally disastrous world conflict. War is no longer an effective instrument of world politics, and our continued existence lies in our ability "to perceive accurately and to respect the widely diversified 'goal values' and 'living laws' of other peoples." The majority of the world's inhabitants still live in status societies as opposed to the modern technological society which is governed by contractual law. The only way to modernize an older society is to impose the new upon the old in such a way as to conform to "the living-law habits of the majority of the community in question."

It is clear that an understanding of other peoples is a task not for a decade, but for a generation — or generations. Not only our national survival, but the continuance of our way of life — or of existence itself — will depend upon how intensively and how well the school educates for intercultural understanding. Such understanding calls for contact with, as well as study about, other peoples. Anthropologist Margaret Mead has said, "You can have education *about* international understanding but not education *in* international understanding without close contact with other peoples of the world." Chester Bowles added another wise word on the approach of intercultural education when he said: "No longer should we stress the quaint, the curious and the deficient in our presentation of other cultures. What we have in common with the aspirations of the people of other cultures is far more important that what divides us."

Communication with and travel to all parts of the world is increasing rapidly regardless of the emphasis in the schools and colleges. The effectiveness of this contact, however, and the fulfillment of the purposes suggested by Northrup depends in large part upon what schools will be doing in this connection within the next few years and beyond. Curriculum planning and consideration by students of their vocational future must take into account the increasing amount of contact that Americans will inevitably have with the other peoples of the world. An understanding of the values of our culture must be developed concurrently with an appreciation of different cultures and the *right* of people in other parts of the world to think and believe differently than we do. Without this, increased contact may mean only increased disdain, friction, and the raw danger of conflict.

The counselor must not only see ahead in time, but also out in space across our planet. Students must be helped to see themselves as world citizens not only through the vision of the teacher and the nature of the curriculum, but through the wisdom of the counselor. Many students of tomorrow will work in other countries for part of their lives. What are the most desirable qualities for such people, the most likely working opportunities? Will the counselor know enough to appreciate social and working conditions in other countries, or will he look with skepticism upon "all strange ways"? He may not only chill the student's expanding interest in the world, he may well lose the student.

*The Either-Or Fallacy*

This section may be unnecessary. It should certainly be brief. What needs to be said with great emphasis, however, is that changing cultural conditions no longer make categorical aims feasible. Aims must be paired or linked. "Vocational" without "intellectual" is simply not realistic in view of the brains emphasis in vocations. It must be intellectual-vocational or vocational-intellectual not one versus the other. Schools *cannot* be intellectual only or vocational only if they would fit into our practical and technological but also ideational and scientific culture.

The same is true for individualization-socialization as a paired aim. One is essential, so is the other. One may be achieved best through the other. And internationalism cannot abandon national awareness and loyalty. One must know how to be an effective American before he becomes the most effective world citizen.

The vocational emphasis, the socialization emphasis, the national emphasis are as essential as ever. But they must be paired in this way: vocational-intellectual, socialization-individualization, American culture-world culture. If we stick to the first concept of each pair, the world will leave us — individually and as a nation — far behind. We shall become, as John Gardner writes, a ". . . museum nation, and tourists from more vigorous lands will come from afar to marvel at our quaint ways."

## The Changing School in Which the Counselor Works

Beyond balancing his time between different student demands and coming to grips with the educational purposes that he should be serving, the counselor must recognize specific changes that are being made within the school structure. He knows full well that he will not be working in "a little red schoolhouse" but neither will he for long be a part of the average school that existed in 1950 or even in 1960. And the counselor must be vitally aware of these transformations if he is to work intelligently with students and relate effectively to teachers and administrators. As much as anyone on the school staff, and more than some, the counselor must be sensitive to the over-all educational climate as it is affected by changes in procedures, organization, and curriculum.

This section will present a selection of changes that are likely to occur within the next decade. In all of these the start has been made. So extensive and so varied is our system of schools — some 26,500 secondary and 95,000 elementary schools — that everything that will be described as an impending change is already in operation in some units of the American school system.

*The Education System as a Whole*

1. *School districts are combining at a rapid rate* so that the total number of school systems is the smallest in our recent history, while the number of pupils has reached an all-time high. The 1959-1960 total of 42,000 school districts is 40 per cent less than it was eight years ago. And the number will continue to decrease. The President's Committee on National Goals recommends that "The approximately 40,000 school districts existing today should be reduced to about 10,000 by 1970."

Larger school districts provide the opportunity for a more adequate physical plant, a more varied and flexible curriculum, and a more specialized staff. Schools grouped administratively within a large district can be interconnected through a communications center. Two-way audio and audio-video systems can connect schools with each other just as classrooms in one school are now connected by a two-way sound system. A two-way audio-video system with many originating points makes the administrative and instructional programs of the school system more flexible as the system grows larger. A larger school system makes possible some of the counselor information sources that are suggested in Chapter 5.

2. *School buildings are becoming more functional in design and more flexible in operation.* The elementary school building of the near future is seen as a one-story building accommodating from 500 to 1,000 pupils with classrooms of varying size and shape designed for different sized groups and different educational functions. Walls will be movable so that the size of the rooms can be adjusted to varying sized groups from year to year or to permit new curriculum concepts to be put into action. Between each two classrooms will be a work laboratory for science instruction and other laboratory work. Such rooms would include booths for individual use of tape recordings and automatic learning machines.

One educational research worker concerned with creative learning in the elementary school (Professor Paul Torrance) visualizes the elementary classroom of the future as a large room with a three-level circular stage around which are the movable desks of the pupils. This arrangement lends itself to a variety of group instructional approaches, demonstrations, role playing, socio-drama, and other face-to-face interactions. The desks can be rearranged into sub-groupings of whatever size is desired. A great deal of wall space is used for display space and storage space for teaching equipment such as tape recorders and teaching machines. Soundproof cubicles are provided at one end of the room and on a balcony for individual learning and small group activities.

The secondary school building also is seen as having various sized rooms for large-group instruction, small-group instruction, and individual study. School buildings generally will have large libraries to permit more individual study and project learning. They will contain laboratories, of course, but also rooms serving as project and material centers, auditoriums, conference rooms, and individual listening-viewing rooms.

3. *That the school plant and staff be utilized for more than the traditional 36 to 38 weeks a year* is now being widely proposed and will be more emphasized in the future. Even now, many school systems are engaging in fairly extensive summer school programs which enable students to engage in remedial work, to take advanced courses, or to take courses which contribute to their social and cultural needs.

The American Association of School Administrators in a 1960 bulletin entitled *Year-Round School* proposes four alternative plans for the better use of plant and staff: (1) the voluntary summer program much as is now in operation in many schools; (2) extension of the regular school year to include an additional 10 to 12 weeks in the summer for professional personnel only, which would enable faculties to keep the instructional programs fresh, revise curricula, and make careful plans for the forthcoming year; (3) a full 48 weeks of school for students and teachers with one month's vacation period, enabling gifted students to complete twelve years' work in nine years, and allowing others to perform at an adequate level over a longer period of time; and (4) a staggered quarter plan for all, with one-fourth of the student population having a vacation each of the four quarters of the year. This would make full use of school plant and personnel, but it would not require the student to attend school longer than nine months.

The last of these plans is probably the most radical and would be the most difficult to put into operation. It would be essential, for example, to be able to divide the total student body into four equal groups in order to have the plant utilized fully by the three-quarters of the group in school at any one time. It would also have the most difficulty in being accepted by families in terms of vacation periods coming at different times during the year. On the other hand, it has been suggested that the present prevailing practice of vacations falling within the summer period exclusively means a crowding of transportation and recreational facilities that could become intolerable in the future.

It would seem that the first three plans have much to commend them. Some combination of these three plans will undoubtedly be in effect in a good many schools within the next few years. Such expanded use of plant and staff focuses upon the more efficient use of the physical facilities of the school system and the provision of a more secure and full professional life for teachers. Of still greater importance, the year-round program makes possible a more flexible program for the benefit of a greater variety of students.

4. *Education that extends beyond the formal school program will undoubtedly increase in the years ahead.* What is now called adult education may be thought of as a continuation-education that will extend throughout much of the lifetime of the individual. This will involve the utilization of school plant and personnel as well as college and university facilities, education programs within industry, and special continuing education programs not yet formulated.

Several recent conferences have stressed the need for this type of adult education in order to bring the present adults up to the level of understanding now possessed by many school and college students. This becomes a process of "catching up." For both the younger and the older, continuation-education is essential in order to "keep up" with the rapid expansion of knowledge and the scientific and technological developments that are so essential a part of everyone's existence. This means regular school and college for varying periods of time, night classes, correspondence courses (don't sell them short particularly for the able and well-motivated student for each lesson returned gets far more individual attention than does a student in a class), courses given by libraries, youth organizations, unions, and employers — a sweeping range of possibilities.

A. A. Liverright, director of the Center for the Study of Liberal Education for Adults, sees four programs of adult education developing in the United States and other parts of the world: (1) the present program of preparation of adults to meet their economic responsibilities as citizens and workers; this is primarily a remedial program for those who have not had an adequate amount of formal education; (2) a continuing technical and vocational education to permit adults to keep up with essential technological and scientific developments which occur during their life span; (3) education for public responsibility that is aimed at providing men and women with facts and information about political, social, and international issues which are of direct concern to them as citizens; and, (4) liberal education aimed at developing the full intellectual and emotional capacities of each individual.

Margaret Mead derives two new educational principles which directly relate to continuation-education. She would conceive of "primary education" in its original sense — that of providing for basic skills in communication, and for an understanding of numbers, geography, transportation, the law, and the nations of the world. This would be expected of all. Beyond this would be "secondary education" in which *the individual would choose the type of knowledge or skill desired and the time when he wished to learn it.* Such learning would take place at various periods throughout his lifetime. Much of this type of education would be carried on within industry or be conducted by agencies of the government other than the public schools and colleges.

A second principle is defined by Mead as "lateral education," that is, learning from one's peers at many periods during one's lifetime, rather than dependence upon a vertical transmission of knowledge from the older person to the younger. She believes that knowledge is expanding so rapidly that much learning must be derived from people who are near the same age and the same point of development as the learner. These somewhat radical modifications of educational concepts stress the need for continuing education throughout one's lifetime by means and emphases that change with the times.

Continuation-education would be affected by an increase in leisure time, but a marked increase seems less likely to come in the reasonable future than is suggested in some popular discussions of the topic. Few adults today have greatly increased their leisure time over the past decade or two. The Twentieth Century Fund suggested that there has been a good bit of loose discussion of increased leisure time and the decreased workweek, because full-time workers have been combined with part-time workers to bring about the figures that are quoted. Their study of full-time workers indicates that there has been a decrease of only three per cent in the workweek for full-time employed workers over the past 20 years, with the current average workweek being between 47 and 48 hours.

It is true that job-released time may increase drastically as a result of some technological or social innovation. This would affect continuation-education, to be sure. But it seems likely that increasing attention to a lifetime program of continuing education will be influenced less by increased leisure time than by other factors. The need to catch up and to keep up vocationally, socially, and culturally is what will commit people generally to a personal program of continuing education. Toynbee cites Denmark as a nation which has developed adult education to a high level in the Danish "high schools" (which are strictly for adults). A Danish farmer will save money for years to be able to take a six-month or twelve-month course and will make it a point of honor to have this raise him culturally rather than economically.

The need for counseling with regard to continuation-education will be very acute. Not only will high school and college counselors need to prepare students for the desirability of such continuing education after their formal "schooling" is completed but many counselors will be needed in the adult education program itself. It is possible that by 1980 counselors for adult education will be in as great demand as were high school counselors in 1960. John W. Gardner has written that "every high school in the land" should provide *continuing educational and vocational counseling for all who leave school short of entering college*, counseling that is available until the former student reaches the age of 21. Perhaps this is the next step in the development of counseling in adult education.

*Changing Procedures Within the School*

1. *A more widespread use of television, radio, and films in instruction* is foreseen for the immediate future. By the spring of 1959, a total of 569 school districts and 117 colleges and universities were making regular use of television for instruction. One of the most significant recent developments is the Midwest Program of Airborne Television Instruction, originating from Purdue University with major support from the Ford Foundation. This is an extensive tryout of educational courses on video tape which is telecast from an airplane flying at high altitude over North Central Indiana. Telecasts, with the first tryout made in May, 1961, cover an area with a radius of 200 miles, embracing 13,000 school and college locations which enroll more than 5,000,000 students. Eventually, from two to six programs will be broadcast simultaneously for six hours each school day.

One-way closed-circuit television has been the subject of experimentation for the past five to ten years with 217 school systems and universities using this form of instruction in 1959. This is likely to increase greatly in scope. Two-way closed-circuit television is also being given serious consideration and is currently in operation in at least one city system. The use of 16 mm. films for instruction is also increasing, with some 700,000 non-theatrical films distributed in 1959 to schools, colleges, and libraries. During that same year 188 educational radio stations broadcast 30,000 programs that were provided by the National Association of Educational Broadcasters.

A long look into the future is provided by Professor John H. Chilcott who wrote on "The Secondary School of 1985" (*The Clearing House*, February, 1960). He proposes that the classrooms of the future will be called learning centers and will contain a good many electronic learning devices for use by individuals or groups. "An English teacher, for example, will be discussing a scene from Shakespeare's *Julius Caesar*. At the appropriate moment she will insert a properly punched card into a slot. A screen will light and the scene under discussion will be enacted by professional actors. At the end of the scene the class will return to its discussion. With learning reinforced in this manner, Shakespeare will virtually "come alive" for the student.

"In a science classroom a student or students may be working on a project concerned with the planet Mars. They will go to a corner of the room, select the correctly punched card, insert it in a slot, and view a complete lecture on the planet, geared to their maturity level and reinforced with many visual aids. In addition to hearing the lecture, the students will be provided with an inexpensive paperbacked study guide which will summarize the lecture, provide additional information, include an annotated bibliography, and suggest further learning experiences in which the students might engage. The study guides will be constructed by a team of subject matter and pedagogical experts in science."

Such a view of the classroom 25 years from now may seem visionary indeed to some people. On the other hand, it may prove conservative in terms of the number or direction of classroom changes that will take place during the next 25 years. At the very least, the present day textbook covering a fairly wide area of knowledge in what is even now a superficial fashion may become obsolete and be replaced by study guides and shorter paperback volumes. The increasing flow of knowledge in any field and the rate of obsolescence involved in textbook material make apparent the need for more frequently appearing study aids of a more specific nature.

2. *Programmed instruction using both mechanized learning units ("teaching machines") and programmed textbooks is certain to influence classroom work in the near future.* Popular attention to the so-called teaching machines has obscured the reasoning back of this new form of instruction. The machine

has been seen as a "monster" which eliminated the need for warm teacher-pupil relationships. (In much the same way, electronic computing machines have been generalized as a threat to the importance of individual workers.) The monster concept has developed from these devices being ineptly labeled "teaching machines"; in actuality, of course, it is not the machine that teaches but the teacher who provides the program for use in the machine. The machine might better be thought of as an individualized or automated learning device.

The learning principles back of this development are simple: (1) the student must take an active rather than a passive role in learning; (2) the material to be learned must be arranged systematically so that each step is built upon the previous one (it is programmed); (3) the learner must be "rewarded" immediately with knowledge of the correctness or error of his answer to the programmed question; (4) the student should proceed at his individual pace with the motivation growing out of step 3. These principles grow directly from Skinner's ideas about learning which were described in Chapter 3.

The automatic nature of the instruction, using either a box-like machine which exposes the material to be learned and the answers or a specially designed book which does the same thing, follows a certain cycle: (1) the student reads a small unit of information exposed by the machine or the book, which calls for a response on his part; (2) he composes a response by filling in a blank, labeling a diagram, or writing a short statement; (3) he is informed of the correct answer while the relevant learning material and his answer are still in view; (4) he advances the program to the next unit. In one of the machines the student *cannot* go to the next item until he has given the right answer — in another the item that next turns up is some additional material on the incorrectly answered response.

It is clear that writing a programmed course for either machine or textbook presentation requires a large outlay of time. Yet the course so designed can be used in all schools of a system by individuals who vary widely in the speed by which they learn. The brighter students can complete a course in half the traditional time and go on to new learnings. One is uncertain how the teacher's role is affected yet the evidence so far suggests that effective programming makes for motivated and creative students. (Two types of programmed texts are illustrated by an elementary psychology book — J. G. Holland and B. F. Skinner, *The Analysis of Behavior* (1961) — and an elementary algebra book — N. A. Crowder and Grace C. Martin, *Adventures in Algebra* (1961).

It seems quite likely that this form of instruction will be used widely in the near future. Lively attention is being given to the development of both automatic programmed devices and programmed texts, with high school curriculum applications being given special attention by the Carnegie-supported Center for Programed Instruction in New York City (365 West End Avenue, New York 24, New York). Free bulletins on its work are available to educators. The counselor should understand the learning principles back of it for they may be the same principles that he will use in counseling (see Chapter 3). He should know too that newer instructional procedures in mathematics and science and the electronic laboratories in the foreign languages are based upon these and other learning principles. The counselor could improve his counseling if he understood and used an effective psychology of learning.

3. *A considerable number of plans for the better utilization of teaching talent* are being experimentally developed in both elementary and high schools throughout the country. Teaching-teams, for example, enable one teacher, perhaps the most competent of the team on a given subject, to present a lecture on a given topic to a number of classes simultaneously. This frees regular classroom teachers for individual work with other students. Some elementary schools, for example, are following a plan that divides pupil time between homeroom teachers who work with them individually and teaching-teams which permit different specialists to pool their efforts for the most effective instructional impact.

A teaching-team, which includes a senior teacher and less experienced teachers, teacher assistants, teaching interns, and nonprofessional teaching aides (J. Lloyd Trump defines the members as professional teacher, instruction assistant, clerical assistant, and general aide), enables each member of the team to do most effectively what he is most competent to do. Special abilities among teachers may thus be used to the full. Such a team concept takes a teacher and his subject out of the isolation of the self-contained classroom. It also varies the work of the teacher during the day and contributes to a greater sense of professional satisfaction. All of this, of course, requires classrooms and auditoriums of varying size for different groupings of students.

One interesting study being conducted at the University of Chicago by Dr. Herbert Thelen is an attempt to provide each teacher with the kind of student with whom he is most effective. This requires that differences in teachers as well as differences in pupils be appraised so that a teacher responding to certain student characteristics is supplied with students possessing those characteristics. Such a plan makes more specific and accurate what counselors frequently do in the normal course of events in helping students to be placed with teachers who may be most effective with that particular student. It seems likely that such type of placement may be made more systematic and this will further involve counselor participation in the process of more adequately matching student to teacher.

4. *The familiar attempt to care in a gross manner for individual differences through so-called ability grouping* is being experimented with in many situations with renewed energy and insight. Grouping upon the basis of general scholastic ability has been tried over the past two or three decades and generally discounted. Parents and students dislike the stigma involved, and it is not psychologically realistic. Each student varies within himself, has large capacity for some kinds of learning or even subjects and less capacity for others. Grouping in terms of a general factor would result in as many inequalities as no grouping at all.

A more flexible plan is the grouping of students in classes in which they have demonstrated subject or skill ability adequate to that class. This means that students may be placed in advanced classes in some subjects and not in others. This greater flexibility will also be more acceptable to students and parents since grouping by subject matter competence is less inclusive than a general labeling of the student as being in an over-all advanced or less advanced sequence of work. Such groupings by ability, whether on individual subject basis or an over-all basis, depend largely on the nature and flexibility of the school curriculum involved.

Grouping of students will eventually be seen in relation to the recognition of different learning values that accrue from large groups, from small groups, and from individualized instruction. A broad divisioning of the school day of the future might see 40 per cent of the pupil's time spent in large group instruction which utilizes the most competent teachers and television instruction, 40 per cent in small group instruction where teachers contribute more intimately to pupil learning and where students learn in group interaction, and 20 per cent in individualized instruction using self-teaching devices, the laboratory, the library, the materials center, etc. The percentages might be different for different subject areas. They might vary for different ability levels with the academically talented, for example, spending more time in individualized study. Such a division of time is not primarily to save time or staff but to provide the kind of learning experience most appropriate to the learning outcome sought.

## Changing Curriculum Patterns

It is difficult to detect the direction of change in the content of school curricula. Curricular modification to meet changing cultural conditions has consisted mainly of redirection and re-emphasis of existing curricular areas. The great influence of Dr. Conant has been directed to "doing better with what we have" rather than with the introduction of new concepts and new meanings.

Schools are becoming more socially effective in emphasizing scientific understanding and the ability to communicate in languages other than English. But it is not too clear whether this emphasis is to be for the production of more scientists and more linguists or the reduction of scientific illiteracy and linguistic provincialism. New attention is being given to the sciences, mathematics, and foreign languages in both elementary school and high school. But the focus of effort seems to be upon the most effective means of reaching these knowledge goals, rather than with the social utilization of the understandings thus achieved.

This is an overstatement, of course. Mathematics and the various sciences, as examples, have been changing markedly as to the concepts involved. These are, however, an outgrowth of changes within the discipline of the knowledge concerned. This is as it should be. What is not taking place is the introduction of new curriculum content to meet changing conditions in our culture as well as meeting changes within an area of knowledge.

This is where the counselor comes in. If, as will be suggested in Chapter 5, the counselor studies changes in the character of the student population and the specific community cultures from which students come, he can supply information upon which curricular changes can be considered. With no pretense at knowing much at all about particular curricular content the counselor can be of great value in the curricular development by supplying information about changing student characteristics and the subcultures of the community. In the paragraphs to follow, four areas of curricular development are described as growing out of projected cultural change. The counselor can help in seeing how these apply to a given school population and community.

1. *If what has been said earlier about the need for greater understanding of other cultures* is accepted as an aim for schools of all levels, then one must conclude that little has been done curriculum-fashion to achieve this objective. It is true that there has been an intensification of language preparation but other areas lag. Geography as an elementary and secondary

school subject certainly deserves greater attention and new content emphasis. To achieve greater intercultural understanding, it would be useful to present history so that a student becomes aware of what has happened in all parts of the world at a given time. He might better appreciate other cultures if he could clearly see how they antedated or paralleled our own. Anthropology and sociology are practically unknown as curricular emphases in the schools, and yet these play a vital part in the understanding of various world cultures and subcultures.

Fred M. Hechinger, education editor of the *New York Times,* wrote that the curriculum for "The Educated Man" would use history and geography to provide a sense of direction, of where man is going in both time and space; that science with its knowledge of the universe would be related to social sciences and history which tell about man and his behavior. In this curriculum, science and technology would be seen as influences in all walks of modern life, intensive reading as essential to cultural survival, and skill in communicating with Americans and with people who use other languages as an integral part of every child's education.

2. Attention is being given to the fact that *students must learn to make wise economic choices and wise family choices.* Consumer education and family life education are fairly recent emphases in the school curriculum. These may be broadened to include a better general understanding of the economic basis of our society and of personal living and of the sociological and psychological bases of the family unit. Education for informed consumer living and wise family living are phases of the substantial curriculum areas of economics, sociology, and psychology.

3. In a rapidly changing and more complex world, there should be *more attention given to the development of a sense of values.* It may be true that values cannot be "taught," but it is certainly true that a sense of values is developed during childhood and the years of adolescence, with or without curricular direction. Professor Kimball Wiles, in discussing the education of adolescents in 1985, believes that one basic element of the high school curriculum of that day will be an area known as Analysis of Meanings and Values. He sees each student spending a block of time each week in an Analysis Group, the purpose of which is to "help each pupil to discover meaning; to develop increased commitment to a set of values, to provide opportunity to examine the conflicts among the many sets of values and viewpoints held by members of society." He proposes this as a basic element of the educational program, for unless

citizens have values they accept, understand, and can apply, the social structure will begin to disintegrate when authoritarian controls are applied. These groups will be taught by emotionally mature people who have been given special training in counselor communication and value analysis. If they attempt "to sell their own viewpoints," they will be considered unsuccessful and be replaced. The pupils bring in questions of ethics, social concern, out-of-school experience, and the implications of knowledge encountered in other classes which become the basic materials for the group learning experience.

An illustration of a recent attempt to introduce new curricular content in the high school was a project supported by the Lilly Endowment Fund, conducted at MacMurray College in connection with the Jacksonville, Illinois, high school. The project introduced a course in Principles of Philosophy in the high school. Three areas of philosophical study were involved: *psychology — who am I?; logic — what is right thinking?; ethics — when is my conduct proper?* Enrollment in the first year was restricted to the upper 12 per cent or less, and stress was placed on great ideas growing out of the study of art, of beauty, of freedom, the concepts of war and peace, of love and justice.

4. Another area in which there appears to be very little in the way of curricular innovation is that of special attention to the *educational needs of girls and young women.* On the whole the American educational system has made little differentiation between boys and girls in curricular emphasis except for courses with direct vocational application. Boys are supposed to take industrial arts and shop work, and girls take home economics and commercial courses. This is no longer sufficient. The changing pattern of women's activities in our society, generally, and in our vocational world, particularly, calls for curricular attention. Women are no longer homemakers only, but carry important civic responsibilities in the community. Increasing proportions are engaging in the work world previously pre-empted by men. It may well be that attention to these changing conditions among women in our society does not call for different curricular content as much as for a broadening of the content of present offerings and more realistic program planning for girls.

*Obsolescence in Knowledge.* This is one uncomfortable characteristic of school curriculum content, of knowledge itself. What is learned almost year by year goes more quickly out of date. Coupled with this is the tendency for the curriculum to be constantly enlarged but seldom pruned. John Ivey called this "curriculum obesity." This regressive tendency to hang on to what is now in the curriculum is in sharp conflict with the need for more rapid curriculum change. One way out, for both counselor and teacher, is to be respectful of the *impermanence* of knowledge, the need to develop in students a constant doubt of the permanence of anything that is learned. What then is to be stressed? The way of finding answers to questions, of knowing the sources of information and how to get facts when needed. No physician can keep up with the drug market and know all the new drugs that have supplanted the older ones. What he does is to know where to look for information when he needs it. What he must learn is a *method* of diagnosis and treatment, not a memorization of all possible diagnoses.

*Utopia?*

In a syndicated article by an Associated Press writer a description is given of "Utopia Union High School District, U.S.A." What is described is more than a dream because every point made is in existence in some or many school systems. This Utopia would have school open for 12 months a year, and the teachers' salaries would be adequate, with no threat of future shortage. Furthermore, there is no classroom shortage because the Utopia School District has 50 portable one-room classrooms that can be moved from school to school as the need arises. Whenever there are as many as six of the portable classrooms at one school a permanent building is erected. The school buildings are all circular with pie-shaped classrooms pointing toward a central auditorium. Wall partitions can be rolled back. There are no windows and no outside distractions. Efficient artificial light and air-conditioning is present in every building.

Attention is given to exceptional children of all sorts and with various forms of adaptations to individual differences. Counselors are provided so that no student is forgotten, and attention is given to various combinations of the conventional curricular areas. Students are introduced to the most effective type of further education.

Throughout the entire article there is no mention of any change in the curriculum as such. If this is a valid cross section, one must conclude that "doing better with what we have" is the rule of the day. It will not be sufficient for tomorrow.

## Beyond High School

That each year will see a larger proportion of high school graduates engaging in some type of education beyond high school seems well assured. The figures have been projected in various studies of which the Department of Labor projection already cited is one. What seems less clear is the *kind* of education in which these students will engage. There is little likelihood that in 1970 the 45 per cent of students of college age who it is said will be engaging in post-high school education will be doing so in colleges and universities as we now understand these institutions. "Liberal arts colleges" and "universities," which meet some reasonable definition of the terms involved, simply do not expand that rapidly without changing character. Nor is it easy to develop within a few years new institutions that are comparable to those already established.

It seems more likely that present institutions will retain their present character and distinctive emphasis or enhance their social contribution in some specific direction. They will be increasingly populated by those who are capable of profiting from the intellectual emphasis of these institutions, simply because there will be a larger supply of such students within the rapidly growing population. This assumes, too, that counselors will improve in their ability to counsel effectively students who will profit from college and that parents and students will be increasingly realistic about college versus other types of post-high school education.

The present loss of student talent is great both at pre-college and within-college levels. Psychologist Ralph Berdie's study of the 1950 situation in Minnesota is probably still representative of 1960 — that for every two exceptionally well-qualified students who were planning to attend college, there was one equally qualified graduate who was not planning on college. (Berdie concludes that so much depends upon parents' attitudes and influence that counselors and the school in general should attempt to be more helpful to parents.) A 1960 study of "honors" seniors in Minnesota high schools (the top two per cent in scholarship) found over one-fourth of them not planning on college.

The loss within college is even more drastic, with Iffert's national study showing that only about 40 per cent of college entrants graduate in four years from the same institution. This proportion increased to 60 per cent for those who ultimately graduated from college and to 70 per cent for those in the upper one-third of their high school graduating class. A loss of 30 to 40 per cent is a poor usage of college facilities, even if you assume that many who failed to graduate still derived some benefit from the experience.

With a larger supply of students upon which to draw, it seems likely that a college will be able to focus on its purposes and select accordingly. This means also modifying its expectations of success. Scholastic attrition in English universities is a cause of alarm when it exceeds 15 per cent. Honors degree students have attrition rates of four and five per cent. The English university *focuses* better and *selects* better than its American counterpart although it is unfair to compare universities in these two cultures in terms of their history, social purpose, or the proportion of the population directly served.

One factor that reduces the effectiveness of any college admissions formula is the uncertainty of a student's scholastic motivation and his particular expectations of college. These undoubtedly affect scholastic performance, and yet they are difficult to use as predictors. Certainly they are interrelated, with student expectation of a particular college affecting motivation for study in that college. The study of student expectations on the one hand and the appraisal of the intellectual and cultural climate provided on a given campus on the other hand is of very recent origin. Such determinations will increase in significance in the future as it becomes more important to waste no college space on the wrong student for that particular college.

The high school counselor has three broad and difficult tasks in helping students — and their parents — on matters of college attendance. The first is to secure acceptance of "the fact of life" that being a college graduate requires qualities of mind not possessed by every high school graduate. Everyone does not have a "right" to be a college graduate any more than everyone has a right to run a four-minute mile.

The second is that colleges vary widely in their intellectual and social climates and a student who will fail in one college will succeed in another even though both may be at the same status level. T. R. McConnell, Paul Heist, and others at the University of California have shown that students of equal ability sort themselves out in some fashion so that on the average those entering one type of college differ in cultural characteristics from these entering another type of college. This may be the influence of friends in a given college drawing like people to them. This could be thought of as wise or unwise, but insuring some degree of "at homeness" on a given campus could be enhanced by knowledgeable high school counseling. Sociologist Martin Trow describes four subcultures found on any campus under the headings of Collegiate (recreation, social), Academic (ideas), Vocational (preparing for a job) and Nonconformist (creative and divergent). A campus wherein one subculture is predominant may mean life for one student and death for another.

The third task for the school counselor is to hold clearly in mind the variety of post-high school educational institutions that are available for students who cannot, or should not, attend college. The number and variety of these will surely increase although the nature of the development cannot be clearly foreseen. One thing is sure — a very unhappy notion is prevalent that college is the only kind of continued learning to be considered. College is not the only path to self-development, and it may well be the *wrong* path for many students.

It should be clear to every counselor that no student leaving school after high school graduation, or before, need to lack in educational opportunity. Although exact figures are lacking, it is likely that in 1960 there were over 50 million enrollments in various types of adult education. Public school adult programs enrolled 3,000,000 at least with a considerably larger number profiting from the evening school, university extension, correspondence (available wherever mail is delivered) and educational TV courses in colleges and universities. There are both vocational and general education opportunities in business and industry programs and in those offered by labor unions — in the 1960 *Handbook of Adult Education* industry and labor each claimed to have the most extensive program of adult education! Libraries, social agencies, and religious institutions, museums and art institutes compete with proprietary (private, fee-charging) vocational schools.

To serve students not planning on college, counselors must know these varied programs and how to evaluate their worth — or know where the information can be found. Education to help him in vocational preparation and in living more richly and fully exists *somewhere* for every student — and most of it is free or nearly so.

In a more specific fashion this section next considers counseling for college under topics of *less well-known colleges, junior colleges, peer influences on college going, girls and college, study abroad, early admissions to college, the widening age-range in college.*

1. *Less well-known colleges.* The variety of colleges and universities in the United States is far greater than in any other country in the world. Of the 1,713 colleges and universities in 1959 that gave undergraduate degrees (of which 328 gave only an Associate in Arts or a similar two-year degree), the school counselor is likely to know less than two dozen. The students know even fewer. Rarely will the student know more than one or two whose characteristics fit his needs and yet there may be from 20 to 100 which he could enter with confidence. Unless the able, but financially lacking, student applies for scholarship aid to several less well-known institutions as well as to the well-

known college of his "first choice," he may never enter college. Yet the less well-known institutions may serve his needs well. This is the counselor's task, to know the institutions well enough to assist the student in the process of choice.

Each year some college spaces go unfilled, excellent "blue ribbon" spaces, because the appropriate student does not know enough to apply there. *Changing Times, the Kiplinger Magazine* for December, 1960, carried the results of its annual survey on openings in colleges still available in the fall of 1960. There were at least 28,000 places open in the various colleges in the country in the fall of 1960, and an anticipated 32,000 openings at the beginning of the second semester. This suggests that because school counselors did not know enough about the colleges involved, some students who planned to attend college did not get to do so.

One way for a student to get a feel of the college that is being considered is to visit the campus while he is a junior or early senior in high school. Over one-half of the students who enter college each year have never been on the campus before they arrive as freshmen. This "mail order" method of choosing a college is unsatisfactory and often expensive. So firmly does one professional organization, the National Vocational Guidance Association, believe in the value of visits that it has prepared and distributed many thousands of copies of *How To Visit Colleges*, a handbook for students, parents, counselors, principals, and teachers. This contains many suggestions on points to consider in choosing a college as well as what can be learned from a visit. A "Choose a College" calendar for the four years of high school is provided. The slogan of the booklet is "He who chooses a college wisely seldom fails to be admitted to a college of his choice."

Excellent, inexpensive booklets for parents were published in 1960 by the American School Counselor Association, *How About College* and *How About College Financing*. These have each gone into several printings, are as useful to prospective college students as to parents, contain timetables for action. (These two associations are divisions of the American Personnel and Guidance Association, and the booklets are distributed by the parent association.)

2. *Junior colleges or community colleges.* These now suffer from lack of prestige, yet many students could have a more satisfying experience in one than to enter a four-year college and be unable to complete the program. The completion of a two-year program which enables the student to identify both with the college and with his own success in it will have a more lasting value than an unsuccessful or minimally satisfy-

ing experience in a four-year college. Yet even in junior colleges the expectation may be unrealistic. One estimate has concluded that three-fourths of the junior college entrants in one large state expect to complete a university transfer program, yet only one-fourth do so. Two-thirds of these students must modify their expectations of themselves, although, to be sure, the new goal may be more rewarding than the former one.

Job opportunities for junior college graduates seem excellent now and in the immediate future if the student will *accept* the opportunities for cultural and vocational development available to him in the two-year program. This again is one of the counselor's tasks — to understand junior college functions, to appreciate the great diversity of such institutions available, to present the student with information that will enable him to appreciate both advantages and disadvantages of two-year colleges. The fulfillment of this task means that the counselor, himself often the recent product of a university graduate school, must well control his own tendency toward academic snobbishness.

The counselor should not consider the junior college a minor factor in the high school student's college plans. In 1959, they enrolled about 25 per cent of all college students, and this proportion will doubtlessly increase.

3. *Peer influences on college-going.* Several factors affect the attitude of high school students toward further education. Basic, of course, is the attitude of parents toward college or toward further education in general. Important also is the degree of academic success experienced during the high school years. More recently studied is the effect of the attitudes of the high school student's age peers.

Sociologist Alan B. Wilson studied the influence of the social climate of a school community upon the educational aspirations of high school boys. In brief, he placed in one group communities in a metropolitan area that were composed predominantly of the homes of professional and white-collar workers — called "A" schools — and into another group; communities inhabited primarily by families whose parents were in the manual and lower white-collar occupations — called "C" schools. It was to be expected, of course, that 80 per cent of the boys in the "A" schools anticipated college as opposed to 38 per cent in the "C" schools.

When Wilson studied within occupational strata, however, he found that the norms of the school society itself modified the attitudes of students. For example, 93 per cent of the sons of professional fathers from the "A" schools planned to attend college, but only 64 per cent of the sons of professional fathers in "C" schools planned on college. It is also assumed that the education of parents influences the college-going aspirations of boys and, of course, it does. In this study, however, 59 per cent of the boys in "A" schools who had fathers with extensive educational backgrounds planned on college, whereas of the boys in "C" schools with similar fathers, only 27 per cent planned on college.

The Class "C" schools were also found to have greater cohesiveness within the student body than the Class "A" schools. The boys from less privileged communities held together much better than did those from more privileged and more cultured communities. This meant that the anti-college influence in the Class "C" schools was more effective in keeping boys from considering college than was the pro-college influence in the Class "A" schools effective in encouraging able boys from less privileged backgrounds to attend college.

This and other studies of the manner in which high school students influence each other indicate that the counselor cannot take some things for granted. He cannot assume that the so-called advantaged student, coming from a home in the middle or upper socio-economic class and perhaps even a home of culture, will not be influenced by what other students in the high school think of the intellectual effort involved and the purpose of college itself. Students may choose not to go to college, may choose a particular college for reasons not associated with the primary purpose of the college itself, may enter college with what are actually non-intellectual attitudes, all primarily because of the intellectual atmosphere of both the home and the high school which they attended. When the high school climate is favorable it is frequently because one or two teachers or counselors have somehow managed to turn the peer group of college-bound seniors away from cars and dates to the excitement of intellectual concerns.

4. *Girls and college.* There are a number of reasons why a smaller proportion of girls plan for and attend college than do boys. This is our history but it will be less so in our future. What is most distressing is that some of the current figures show that the greatest gap between the proportions of boys and girls entering college is among upper ability students. A study undertaken by Donald S. Bridgman for the National Science Foundation found that 85 per cent of the male high school graduates who were in the upper 30 per cent in high school ability attended college as compared to 55 per cent of the girls in the same ability range. Of the boys in the upper 10 per cent of ability, 94 per cent attended college compared to 61 per cent of the girls. It is true that the proportion of girls attending college is slowly increasing, but counselors must be aware of

the very real need for considering women in college as an important social and labor force resource.

It has been earlier pointed out that women will enter the labor force in an increasing number during the next decade, both married and unmarried women. It is important that the intellectual abilities of women be respected as highly as those of men and that their admission to college be given the same encouragement. John W. Gardner, in *Goals for Americans,* writes that girls at all ages should be actively encouraged to develop their intellectual capacities. Women are entering the professions very slowly with only 10 per cent of the Ph.D.'s being granted to women. "Such a waste of talent is a relic of the past. We can afford it no longer." All who work with girls should know that "women are capable of advanced education in any field, including mathematics, science, engineering, medicine, and law. . . . Colleges and graduate schools should make it easy for women to continue their education part-time (or to interrupt it) during the period of heaviest family obligations."

Women will continue to attend college because they wish to find prospective husbands who are congenial to their cultural level. They will have an increasing opportunity to attend college because the opportunities for them in the professional and vocational world will be attractive. This may be accompanied by marriage or not. But the high school counselors should feel responsible for helping girls to see that their social and vocational responsibility is fast equaling that of men. And that their plans for college should be considered accordingly

5. *Study abroad.* For high school counselors who have not themselves traveled beyond their own country, it will seem a little unrealistic to assume that many students who go to college will study abroad or travel abroad during the period of their college experience. In 1960 at least 15,000 American students were studying in other countries, 5,000 of them in 85 branches of American colleges and universities. This is certain to expand rapidly. Not only this, of course, but men and women of the future will work at their vocation in many parts of the world.

It would seem important that high school counselors are informed on the various plans for summer student travel and that they become familiar with the various opportunities for study abroad during the regular academic year. The reality of the closeness of our hemisphere to the rest of the world should influence choice of courses, and, in particular, an understanding of other cultures and their languages. Provision for this kind of "thinking ahead" will affect the curriculum in the junior high school as well, for it is proposed that languages may well

103

begin at this level. (More so in the future than in the past, attendance in college will be integrated with experience within a metropolitan area as well as affording contact with other cultures. If the assumption is correct that college and university students will increasingly be in intimate contact with urban life, either directly or by field study with the urban area, then, in general, the ivory-tower concept of the college held by many counselors will have to be modified.)

School counselors should recognize that college-age youth may well not only study abroad or work abroad but wish to *serve* abroad. Many young people want to make their world into a more effective world than the one this generation bequeaths to them. Harold Taylor writes "We have been talking about educating the young for a world they have already outgrown while they have been talking privately about a world they wish to bring about."

The National Peace Corps, first proposed in 1960 by Representative Reuss and the late Senator Neuberger and advocated in the presidential campaign of President Kennedy, received quick attention from many college groups. The opportunity to apply their newly acquired skills and knowledge for the betterment of people in the "developing" countries of the world has appealed to thousands of college young people. Projects developed early at Harvard and the Massachusetts Institute of Technology resulted in the appearance of 350 applicants for the 20 opportunities to teach in Nigeria. At the University of Michigan 10,000 students turned out at two a.m. to hear candidate Kennedy speak of the need for public service abroad and went into immediate plans for a Youth Peace Corps. More recently has been proposed an International Youth movement under the United Nations with the suggested name of Youth Cadres for Peace. It is more than possible that the rest of the world and its needs seem more real to youth than it does to adults. This kind of practical idealism, an informed and imaginative realism, can be seen in embryo among high school students as well, if counselors are capable of seeing the dream with them. College then becomes a place where one learns not only to do but to do *for* someone, to have a reason for being.

6. *Early admissions and cooperative admissions.* If school counselors are to become effective in the transition between high school and further education, they must become students of college admission plans. These will vary widely, and the changes to be made in the near future are as yet only dimly seen. It is certain, however, that colleges and universities having selective admissions will move toward an earlier admissions date than had been true in the past. There is a tendency among some high

schools to engage in cooperative plans for securing psychometric data during the junior year in high school so that college planning can be started early. This will result in colleges and universities utilizing these data to make student acceptance known by the middle of the high school senior year or earlier. Such action will be an advantage both to the college and to the student because the student is thus enabled to move from an early knowledge of nonacceptance in a given college to application to another institution. As liberal arts colleges and universities are enabled to become more selective, the early admissions policy will become increasingly effective, and high school students will start specific college planning no later than the middle of the junior year in high school.

The Cooperative Plan for Guidance Admission, which has just been initiated by the Educational Testing Service, is an indication of the kind of broad scale admissions operation that will be increasingly utilized. The Cooperative Plan (recently inaugurated in the State of Georgia) enables a group of colleges to come to an understanding with high schools regarding the information that is to be made available to all the colleges in the Plan. The material is electronically processed with all the information returned to the high school for use during the senior year for counseling purposes. When the student wishes to apply for admission to college, the school will enter his senior year grades and additional test scores on a Comprehensive Student Report, and one of the multiple copies of the report can then be torn off and sent by the school to each of the colleges to which the student is applying. The same information may be used in providing information to prospective employers.

Increasingly, such broad-gauged cooperative planning will become essential as the information required for the most effective admissions becomes more complex, and at the same time it becomes more possible to analyze and process such information through the use of electronic devices. Such a system makes more information available about the student than is now used in most admissions and employment decisions. And so the record on the student becomes a more complete picture of the individual as he exists. This is an illustration of the fact that long-range planning using electronic computers can represent the individual more completely — the whole process becomes more personal rather than more impersonal.

7. *Widening age-range in college.* The counselor should be constantly alert to the fact that college is "not like it was when I was there!" One illustration is that the age-range is wider, with only 60 per cent of the students in 1959 falling within the "normal" age-range of 18 to 21 years of age. About six per cent

were 16 to 17 years old but the rest were older. So the new freshmen will find many older students on a campus, particularly on a university campus where the bulk of the graduate school students will fall within the 25 to 35 age-range. A National Science Foundation report on science Ph.D.'s granted in 1958 and 1959 gave an average age of 31½ years at the time the doctorate was given. The mean lapse of time between baccalaureate degree and doctorate was eight years.

With an anticipated increase in the number of people returning to regular college campuses as well as special institutes for "refresher" work, more older students will be seen on the average campus. Many wives and husbands are on campus also. In 1959, 30 per cent of men and 13 per cent of women college students were married so that the freshmen will be rubbing elbows not only with older but with "family" students as well. This may contribute to the freshman's speedier maturation — it may result in a defensive reliance upon the companionship of his own age peers and a retardation of his development.

## Conclusion for the Counselor

Thus far the report has reviewed anticipated changes in the world culture as it touches upon America, changes in the American culture, and changes in the subculture of the educational world, with an excursion into developments in psychology. If the counselor-reader or other reader is not yet impressed with the counselor's need for knowing the settings in which he operates as well as the students with whom he deals, such reader had better stop now. Read no further for it will be of little advantage to you. The writer and the Commission have failed.

A summary of this chapter would appear unwieldy and unnecessary. American education is viable and vital, critics to the contrary. There should be a glow of pride in each of us regarding American education's past and present and the great concern of the public in this endeavor. There is some justifiable apprehension, however, that education (schools, boards, professionals, parents) will not move rapidly enough to keep pace. Such failure will be as fatal as military unpreparedness.

In all of this, the counselor plays a part. Knowledge of students, of school purposes and aims to which he owes allegiance, of the school organization and of procedures that surround him immediately and every day, of next steps in education, are crucial to the carrying out of his school functions. And the impression of accelerating change is here too. The counselor can be left behind in the changing school.

Chapter 5

# *The School Counselor's Task*

# The School Counselor's Task

## CONTENTS

## It Is Recommended:

1. That the counselor recognize that of the multifold functions of the school in developing intellectual, social, and vocational competencies the primary and most unique function of the school is that of the development and use of the intellect; that he ally himself with this intellectual core effort as he works with both students and staff.

2. That primary emphasis in counseling students be placed on the developmental needs and decision points in the lives of the total range of students rather than upon the remedial needs and the crisis points in the lives of a few students, with the major goal of counseling being that of increased self-responsibility and an increased maturity in decision-making upon the part of the student.

3. That the school counselor attempt to keep abreast of changes in the occupational community and in the world culture into which a student will move. This can be approached through the reading of at least one book or two reports a year in each of these areas: labor force changes and projections; family life; governmental responsibility; the nature of the American economy; and intercultural or world culture developments.

4. That problems of motivation, aptitude, and learning be seen as basic and interrelated aspects of human behavior about which the school counselor must be informed substantially beyond the point of popular understandings.

5. That counselors understand that they tend to be security-oriented, in part because they relate themselves more easily to the past than to the future, in part because they safeguard their influential relationship with students in the direction of "safe" decisions. But safety for the present may mean disaster for the future. Counselors need to balance undue caution with a risk-taking orientation which will encourage students to look to the future and to dare to be intellectual and vocational pioneers.

6. That vocational choice be seen as a process extending over years and not as an event, that the student be helped to make a series of choices as he becomes increasingly realistic about himself and the occupational world, that urging a student to "make up his mind" in the sense of a final settlement may be considerably more harmful than helpful.

7. That the recognition and encouragement of latent talent and creativeness be understood to require tools and understandings of a special sort which the counselor must actively develop. This takes self-understanding and courage upon the part of the counselor because the talented student who is creative and intellectually unconventional may be something of a threat to the teacher and the counselor. Parents, too, need understanding and encouragement as they relate themselves to the child's often unexpected and singular talents.

8. That the school counselor's understanding of human behavior and of the other person's need for acceptance and encouragement be at the disposal not only of students but of teaching colleagues, administrators, and parents. In being directly helpful to them he is indirectly helpful to the students whom they influence.

# The School Counselor's Task

THIS REPORT is about the counselor but it is clear that he does not operate in a vacuum. He works within a changing culture, uses perceptions of human behavior that are constantly modified as new research is considered, is an employee of a school whose evolution and function he must understand. One major theme of this report is that the future development of counseling can be understood only as changes within society, psychology, and the school are understood. For this reason the second half of the report is based solidly upon the first half rather than upon armchair reasoning as to what counselors *should* do. It is based upon what it is apparent that they must do to be effective in the changing picture.

A second theme of this report is that the counselor is the major factor in the effectiveness of any pupil personnel program and the program is best seen in relation to him. If his function is clear, the balance of the "guidance" picture falls into perspective. This report considers the guidance program but after it has become clear on the nature of the counselor's job. It is easy to wax eloquent on a "program" but it is people who carry out the program. So consideration is given first to the counselor and his relation to students, teachers, parents, and administrators. All of these perform some guidance functions, all can be helped by a counselor who knows his job and knows his relation to the others who work with the student.

Earlier chapters have suggested what the counselor needs to do in response to the changing cultural and educational scene. Some of his specific tasks are clear such as those considered in the last part of the preceding chapter, *i.e.*, assistance to the student in planning for the next educational step. The job ahead that grows out of societal conditions will not be forgotten but the next concern is an analysis of what counselors *presently do* and what they think counselors *should do in the future*.

## Studies of Counselors

The Commission utilized data from two studies of secondary school counselors and one of elementary school counselors. Two of these were studies specifically completed for this report: (a) a 10 per cent random sample of the active members of the American School Counselor Association (ASCA) who were in

1960 working in secondary schools; and (b) a "cluster" sample of elementary school counselors.

A third source of information was Project TALENT (The Identification, Development, and Utilization of Human Talents, a project of the American Institute for Research, under the sponsorship of the U. S. Office of Education). The main burden of this nationwide study was an extensive testing of the talents of some 440,000 high school seniors, but data were also systematically gathered on counselors, the guidance program and the school program. The raw data from the Project TALENT Study first became available in the fall of 1960. When it was apparent that the complete analysis would take a considerable period of time, the Commission asked for early access to the information on the guidance program and the school counselors. Cooperation from the TALENT staff, in particular Dr. John C. Flanagan, Dr. John T. Dailey, and Dr. Isadore Goldberg, was unreserved and as a consequence this careful national sample of secondary school guidance work is being given early publication. The data reported here are from 808 public secondary schools, exclusive of separate junior high schools, representing an 89 per cent response to a 5 per cent stratified random sample of high schools throughout the country.

The two secondary school studies, the Commission's ASCA study and Project TALENT, dealt with different groups of counselors. Members of the American School Counselor Association have met the membership requirements of 15 hours of graduate work in professional courses and current employment for at least one-third of their time in work directly related to the guidance program. These are not very stringent professional requirements, but this group contains the best qualified group of counselors available for study on a national basis. As will be seen, most of the members have qualifications considerably in excess of this minimum.

On the other hand, the TALENT Study was a random sample of high schools in which all personnel who gave 20 per cent or more of their time to any part of the guidance program were considered to be counselors and were asked to complete the Study schedule for that group. Since the studies were also designed for different purposes (the ASCA Study was an analysis of the reactions of a selected group of high school counselors to their present work and their projection of it into the future while the TALENT Study was a description of what counselors in senior high schools at all levels of preparation are now doing) there are few points of overlap in the instruments used.

The sampling of elementary school counselors is not as good as for the two groups of secondary school counselors. There

112

is no national association of elmentary school counselors from which to draw (many belong to ASCA), and it was difficult to determine just where counselors in elementary schools are located. A rough cluster-sampling approach was used in an attempt to secure the reactions of a representative number of counselors in each of several areas where elementary school counselors could readily be identified and reached. Elementary school counselors in the states of Missouri and Connecticut, and in the cities of Philadelphia and Baltimore on the East Coast, and Los Angeles (County), Long Beach, and Bakersfield on the West Coast were sent forms similar to those used for the ASCA Study. The 71 per cent response was not what one would like, but it is the best that is available on a national scale. The existing literature revealed little of the sort of information provided in this study.

*Present-Day Counselors — Who They Are and What They Do*

1. The high school counselor is slightly more likely to be male while two-thirds of the elementary school counselors are female. (Table 1 on page 192 gives more exact figures on this and related information.)

2. The median age is slightly above 40.

3. A substantial majority of each group have the master's degree (Table 1).

4. The most typical counselor in the Project TALENT Study has an employed school term of 10 months (47 per cent) with 27 per cent having 9 months and 15 per cent a 12-month appointment.

5. The salaries reported for the Project TALENT counselors are as follows:

| Yearly Salary of Under | Per Cent of Counselors |
|---|---|
| $4,000 | 9 |
| 4,500 | 15 |
| 5,500 | 22 |
| 6,500 | 26 |
| 7,500 | 18 |
| over    8,000 | 10 |

The median would appear to be in the neighborhood of $6,000, but there are wide differences reflected by size and type of school. The median salary increases about $1,000 in moving from small schools (graduating class of under 100) to medium-sized, and from medium-sized to large schools (over 400 in graduating class). Likewise the median increases about $1,000 when moving from the kindergarten-through-grade-12 type school to the six-year high school and from the six-year high school to the three- or four-year senior high school.

113

6. Slightly over half of the secondary school counselors work in three- to four-year senior high schools and these are the larger schools of this type (Table 1). Three-fourths of the elementary school counselors of this study work in grades 1-6 only.

7. High school counselors (ASCA study only) have student loads ranging from less than 100 students per counselor to over 1,000. The median counselor-student ratio is 1 to 412 students. Over 10 per cent are in schools with ratios of 1 to over 1,000.

The elementary school counselor range is similar but the median ratio is 1 to 690 students. One-third have responsibility for more than 1,000 students. As indicated in Table 1 these counselors frequently are responsible for more than one school.

8. The most frequently used title is "counselor" but the variation is wide (Table 1).

*What Counselors Do in the Schools.* 1. Almost all elementary school counselors (98 per cent) are assigned full time to various phases of existing guidance programs and the same is true for a substantial majority (73 per cent) of the ASCA secondary counselors. The proportion of full-time assignment drops sharply to 20 per cent for the TALENT group of high school counselors.

2. When the Project TALENT data are examined by schools, and they represent a fairly accurate cross section of the high schools of the country, we find that 27 per cent of these schools have no counselors at all. In 46 per cent of the schools no one is assigned full time to "guidance duties." As would be expected, the larger schools and the senior high schools are most frequently served by full-time people. Not all listed by the principals and guidance directors are counselors, however, since the principals' blanks on guidance programs report more than twice as many "guidance workers" as are reported on the counselor's blanks as "counselors." Principals consider themselves, teachers who administer tests, core curriculum teachers, and many others as "guidance workers." So they are, but the concept of guidance thus becomes quite widely diffused.

3. From one-fourth to one-third of the full-time counselors in the ASCA and elementary school groups devote one-half time or more to counseling students (Table 1). None spends full time with students. The data for the TALENT counselors are not quite comparable but we find here that only 15 per cent of all counselors in the smaller schools devote half time or more (of whatever time they have) to counseling students as compared to 64 per cent in the largest schools. About one-fourth

of all counselors spend over half of the time they are assigned to "guidance duties" in teaching, rollroom or homeroom duties. and straight administrative tasks. (Table 2 on page 193 provides additional information.) The term "guidance" becomes very fuzzy indeed.

The TALENT Study (and not the other two) provides information on the senior high school counselor's ranking of frequency of counseling and other school duties. The counseling duties ranking highest in frequency for these schools are clearly those of "counseling for college" and "counseling for high school program." ("Administering tests" and "teaching" are related duties taking almost as much time.) Also high in counseling duties, but about half as frequently as for the top two, are "counseling for developing potential" and "counseling for inadequate achievement." Still lower is "counseling for occupations." All of these are responses to a checklist so, to some degree, the items are suggested by the items on the form. The interpretation of what is meant by an item therefore may vary, but the low ranking of vocational counseling suggests a disturbing absence of what many assume to be a vital counseling area for adolescents.

"Counseling for college" in the three- to four-year senior high school is extremely high in frequency, twice as frequent as the next highest item, and 11 times as frequent as "counseling for developing potential." On the other hand, "counseling for occupations" ranks much lower than other counseling emphases in the three- to four-year senior high school, increasing somewhat in significance in the six-year high school.

4. Almost twice the proportion of elementary school counselors as ASCA counselors spend two periods or more a day consulting with teachers and parents (Table 1). On the other hand, more high school counselors do group work with students. Apparently more time is spent by both groups in program mechanics and clerical work than in group work. Not included in Table 1 is the information that the TALENT counselors spend a larger *proportion* of their time in mechanics and clerical work than the other two groups. They are scattered more thinly and yet they spend more time on the impersonal phases of the program. Coupling these facts with the earlier finding that in the smaller schools less counselor time is spent with students, one has a feeling that as total counselor time decreases so decreases the proportion of time given to students. "For to every one who has, more will be given" would apparently apply to the opportunity that a student has of being able to see a counselor.

*Illustrations from Elementary Schools.* The distinctive flavor of the work of the elementary school counselor may be better appreciated through illustrations from two city school systems, neither of which were included in the Commission's studies. The first of these is a description solicited by the writer of the work of the Adjustment Teacher (who elsewhere might be known as an elementary school counselor) in the Leander Stone Elementary School in Chicago. The variation in the program provided by different schools is well illustrated since this title for a counselor is distinctive for the Chicago schools and more attention is apparently given to group work than is true in other schools. The principal of the school, Miss Celia Rosenzweig, writes:

> Each member of the faculty is concerned with helping each child to help himself and with providing conditions favorable for growth. In this manner each teacher is seen as concerned with both group guidance and with the counseling of children and parents. The Adjustment Teacher coordinates the efforts of all members of the staff and works directly with children as individuals and in groups.

> A summary of the program follows:

### Group Guidance

A. Assisting children to evaluate their own growth through interpretation of profiles of test results.
B. Helping 8A's to evaluate the past and to plan for the future by providing them with information that will help them make wise choices and decisions (a three-week program preceding parent-interviews).
  1. Use a unit called "What Do You Know About Yourself?"
  2. As the unit "Planning a High School Program" is developed, the brochure *What Next* and publications which list college requirements are studied.
  3. Provide for parent interviews.

### Individual Counseling

A. Conference with teacher, initiated by teacher or the Adjustment Teacher, to select children who need tutoring.
B. Interviews with teachers, parents, and/or children in order to provide assistance to children who have academic deficiencies and/or social, emotional, or health problems.
C. Counseling children who initiate the interview by requesting the conference.

The second illustration is from the well-written description of the situation in New York City, *Guidance of Children in the Elementary Schools.* This complete description of the elementary school program in a city which has recently carried out several innovations in both elementary and high school counseling contains excerpts from the daily logs of 25 guidance coordinators working in the elementary schools of New York City in 1956. Each works in a different district of the city and each serves a number of schools. In one part of the report excerpts are given from the logs of 25 coordinators on what they were doing at ten o'clock in the morning on the same given day. Comments from the logs of 13 of the coordinators are summarized here:

1. Observed Joseph in class at teacher's request. Noted behavior. Conferred with teacher. Suggested more extensive planned observation and use of anecdotal record for the next few weeks before referral to the Bureau of Child Guidance.

2. Read story to children in third-year class and discussed guidance implications. Discussed results with teacher.

3. Conference with president of Parents' Association in reference to film to be shown at evening meeting. Asked me to serve as discussion leader. I accepted.

4. Spoke to teacher, Miss K., who has a personal problem. Gave support.

5. Counseled Robert and Frank on choice of high schools.

6. Conference with assistant superintendent to plan district-wide meeting on coordinating the services of curriculum, guidance, and health personnel.

7. District-wide meeting of Parents with Advanced Training. Led discussion on *Permissive Behavior versus Discipline*.

8. Interview with Paul M. (8-2) at the request of the principal. Paul is a truant. Discussed reasons and worked out a tentative plan together. Paul and I made an appointment for a second interview.

9. Conference with school nurse about Betsy. Will arrange for hearing test.

10. Interviewed a mother and interpreted clinic services in Brooklyn Jewish Hospital. Phoned Pediatric Clinic of hospital and made appointment for parent.

11. Previewed with the eighth-year teachers (while their classes were in the auditorium) the filmstrips *Classification of Occupations* and *Professional and Managerial Occupations*. They liked the material covered and the arrangement of each filmstrip, and planned to show to their classes.

12. Conferred with kindergarten teacher regarding Amos O. whose mother I interviewed last week because he was

not making satisfactory social adjustment in his class. Teacher says she has been giving Amos little jobs to do and that he seems to be much happier and has fewer spats with other children.

13. Helped Mr. Evans, 2–4 teacher, construct sociogram of his class.

From these and other programs it is clear that the duties of an elementary school counselor vary widely as to title and emphasis, even more so than in secondary school. In some areas the work done by the elementary school counselor is inseparable from that done in other situations by school social workers or school psychologists. In city or county systems where school social workers and school psychologists as well as counselors are employed, the elementary school counselor is likely to be the individual coordinating the work of the various specialists as they work with staff and students.

*What Counselors Want to Do*

The counselors in both the Secondary (ASCA) and the Elementary Counselor study were asked these open-ended questions:

1. Which of your *present activities* as a counselor are *so basic* that they should be maintained even with changed social and educational conditions that might be anticipated during the next 20 years?

2. Which of your *present activities* do not belong in a guidance program even though they may be part of the total administrative or instructional functions? Another way of stating this is to say that these are not the duties of a counselor or guidance worker. (Please name *specific* activities.)

The categorization and the tabulation of their free-response answers reveals some expected emphases and some conditions that are less expected. (Tabulated data are found in Table 3 on page 194.) It is not surprising that a larger proportion of secondary school counselors than of those in the elementary school emphasize the counseling of students as the most basic of their activities to be maintained. The elementary school counselor, on the other hand, would focus more than the secondary school counselor on working with parents and teachers. They are also considerably less interested in furthering group guidance and orientation activities and more interested in using community agencies for referral purposes. These differences may suggest basic differences in the needs of elementary school youngsters and in the qualifications of the teaching staff as well as reflecting the kind of person presently engaged in elementary school counseling. More will be said of this later.

118

When one looks at the activities that the counselors think should not be carried forward or that are not legitimate responsibilities of the counselor, one notes that twice as many elementary school counselors as secondary school counselors find nothing wrong with their present situation or at least nothing wrong enough to be specified in a statement. It is also clear that clerical work troubles many more secondary school counselors than elementary school counselors. When one-half of these counselors respond saying, in effect, that this type of work keeps them from doing what they think could be more significant, it would seem that there is something quite wrong in the perception that the principal and superintendent, and perhaps the school board, have of the function of the counselor.

The fact that in general a smaller percentage of the elementary school counselors are engaged in activities that they do not think legitimate for their function should be encouraging for those interested in developing more effective counseling in the elementary school. In only one "should not do" category is there a larger proportion of elementary school than high school counselors. About equal proportions of elementary and secondary school counselors object to the use of counselor time for class sponsorship, study hall supervision, routine discipline, and the mechanics of psychological testing.

In some of these areas, discipline for example, professionals in both teaching and counseling must be involved, but it is a mistake to use either for routine discipline mechanics. It is also a mistake to have an administrative policy which requires counselors to be responsible for study hall and detention hall supervision, or which requires $6,000-a-year counselors to do $3,000-a-year clerical jobs.

## What Counselors Will Be Expected To Do in the Future

Answers to this question need to be sought from several sources, but, again, the counselors themselves should be asked first. Questions bearing on future developments were asked of both groups of counselors who were asked to assist in the Commission Study, but questions differed for the two groups and their responses should be examined separately.

*Secondary School Counselors (ASCA Members)*

These counselors were asked the following free response questions:

> Try to imagine the nature of society and of the schools in 1980 and list under the headings below what will be happening 20 years from now. Dream a little, not about the ideal, but about the reality of counseling 20 years hence.

Anchor your dreams to an assumed future reality as much as you can, conveniently, but don't let this restrict your imagination!

(a) Basic activities for the counselor in 1980?

(b) Counselor competencies and preparation 20 years from now?

(c) Changes in the emphasis and objectives of counseling?

It is clear that a given counselor could make one or a dozen suggestions under Question (a). As a consequence any percentages given here will be in terms of the ratio of the responses falling in a given category to the total number of responses made by all counselors.

Under (a), a total of 638 suggestions were given and of these 57 per cent bore on *counseling with students*. This makes it very clear that when a high school counselor thinks of the future of his function he thinks of it primarily in terms of working with students on a counseling basis. Some imagination was shown, with about 10 per cent of the suggestions given specifying counseling based upon various types of mechanical supports such as electronic computers, the use of records that can be televised from room to room, and the use of occupational information that has been collected in a center and interpreted for schools as rapidly as changes take place.

Again 10 per cent of the suggestions specify *counseling which relies upon other resources* such as various professional specialists and systematized knowledge of social, vocational, and international conditions. With this look into the future, *vocational counseling* ranks highest of all of the kinds of specialized counseling, representing about eight per cent of the total suggestions. Conferences with or *counseling of parents* is as frequently listed in their projections of the future as is *identification of specialized talent*.

*Work with groups* has one-seventh as many suggestions made as were made for counseling, but it is the category with the highest number of responses of any of those falling outside of the category of counseling with individual students.

*Elementary School Counselors*

They were asked these questions:

Assuming that current concerns in counseling will continue to be emphasized — early identification and motivation of the talented on the one hand and the pre-delinquent on the other, vocational counseling of those in elementary school who may leave school early, etc. — do you see counseling in elementary schools during the next 20 years moving toward (1) the more clinical emphasis on psychological diagnosis and assistance for exceptional and atypical children or (2) the counselor serving as a coordinator of many counseling facilities in the school and community, with more time spent in helping parents and teachers than individual children? Or what emphasis for the future?

  (a) In order to achieve the above, what conditions in school need to be changed?

  (b) In order to achieve the above, what elementary school counselor competencies should be emphasized during the next 20 years? What emphasis in graduate education?

  (c) What should become the elementary school teacher's role with pupils as compared with the counselor's role?

In response to the major question, it is clear that the majority of elementary school counselors believe that Alternative 2 would predominate during the next decade or two, with 45 per cent choosing Alternative 2, and 32 per cent indicating some combination of 1 and 2. Only 23 per cent specified the more strictly clinical emphasis. This question is of major concern at the elementary school level as opposed to the high school level because teachers bear a somewhat different relationship to their pupils in the elementary school than in the high school. There is also greater use of school psychologists and school social workers. The generalization may be drawn that the majority of these counselors see their function in the future being that of spending more time in the coordination of counseling facilities in school and community and in helping parents and teachers than in working clinically with individual children.

The responses of this group were widely varied regarding the changes that they perceive the school needs to make in order to provide for a more effective counseling function. Between 10 and 20 per cent of the counselors specified the need for (a) *better definition of the function of the guidance program* to parents, teachers, administrators, and community; (b) more inservice courses for teachers which would contribute to the *teacher's better understanding of the work of the counselor* and other phases of the guidance program; (c) more emphasis in *teacher education upon human relations* and the dynamics of behavior; (d) *a smaller case-load per counselor* with more secretarial and clerical assistance; (e) greater resources provided by the school in the form of *other professional staff* such as social workers, psychologists, and psychometrists.

(Their responses on the question regarding counselor preparation and competencies will be considered in the last chapter of the report.)

In response to Question (c) these counselors tended to see their function as that of a resource person for teachers and administrators combined with service to individual pupils and parents. They stressed *the teacher's role* as including responsibility for counseling and other guidance services for the majority of students, for instruction and discipline, for sharing with the counselors the work that is done with parents, and for the use of group techniques in securing better individual understanding and social adjustment of students.

Many of the free-response answers to questions cited in these two studies deserve to be quoted in full. Two or three excerpts from each of the two groups of counselor responses suggest the flavor of some of the more imaginative of the groups.

*Secondary School Counselors.* "If survival of groups comes to depend upon producing the 'best team' — as in sports — emphasis will shift to identification of talented individuals and development of such talents in terms of the interest of the group, rather than of the individual. Counselors then would have the duty of getting the maximum usage (from the group's point of view) out of each individual according to the needs of the group. Since the foregoing forecasts the obliteration of democracy as we know it, my *foremost concern* as a counselor is to protect and preserve the interests of the individual no matter what happens. May I suggest that this problem of conflict between the need for self-preservation through meeting the objectives of the group and the need to preserve the individual, as such, be given appropriate consideration in attempting to project the future of counseling."

"Counselors will have much better tools to work with in 1980. Such things as electric scoring and sorting machines will release the counselor to do more research, spend less time with each counselee, and to see more students in a more adequate fashion."

"More contacts with parents, and more contacts with classes. Counselor given much more training and preparation. Counselor given more opportunity to observe regular teaching in every grade from first to 12th, even for a few days in each. Objectives must still be that of helping individual to attain self-understanding, to be a source of information, to promote the counselee's understanding of situations."

*Elementary School Counselors.* "Roles are assumed according to training and experience. At present, at least, the possibility of expecting each teacher to have a counselor's training would seem to be financially out of bounds for all schools except those which have producing oil wells on the campus. More formal course work in growth and development should be required for all, and more rigid standards should generally be set for counselors' certificates. Behavioral deviations at the lower levels of severity would be handled by teachers, at the upper levels of severity by psychologists and psychiatrists (outside agencies) and the levels in between by the counselors. This earth-shaking proposal poses the question as to where and how these limits or levels of severity be determined. Intraprofessional and interprofessional agreement would seem desirable, but at the present unlikely."

"The elementary teacher's role will be exactly what it is today — primary responsibility for the educational and social growth of the children in his class. The guidance service will continue to have as its primary function, service to individual youngsters directly and through service to their teachers and their parents."

"More resources for the children in the form of psychologists, social workers, reading consultants. There ought to be a greater awareness on the part of the community as to school needs and the effect of community patterns on the children. Recognition that the school cannot do the job alone."

## Responses from Counselor-Educators

Turning from the responses of counselors, the Commission sought to secure the reaction of a selected group of graduate professors currently responsible for counselor education. This was not a representative group but was a sample of the better-known people in the field. These men and women gave generously of their time with 32 responding individually to that part of the ASCA counselor form that dealt with their expectations for the future. In addition, five panels of counselor-educators and other professional personnel were held in different sections of the country. They provided a rich reservoir of ideas from which the writer drew not only for the brief report of this section but for some of the generalizations to be made later.

Some of the responses grouped themselves in categories similar to those suggested by the counselors themselves. For example, practically all stated that a considerable proportion of the counselor's daily time should be spent in working with the students, that more time should be given to colleague relationships within the school, that less time be given to the mechanical aspects of the task.

1. There was a considerable stress on counselors becoming well informed on *student developmental needs* and on the decisions to be made by students from time to time in their school program.

One psychologist stated it as follows:

The counselor is to be thoroughly familiar with the developmental process in the life of each student and to

123

intervene in just those cases where he can see the possibility of helping a desirable process along.

Another commented:

> Counseling had a bad start when we organized guidance
> as an information-dispensing function on the one hand or
> as a diagnostic objective measurement function on the
> other hand. We could borrow the model of the child guid-
> ance clinic and not restrict it to the abnormal and atypical.
> Then the counselor would be seen as one who knows more
> about human development, and human problems, than does
> anyone else in the school. In the case of the child guidance
> elementary school clinic, this is now true.

And still another:

> The new emphasis will be on the positive development
> of attitudes, value systems, adjustment skills and competen-
> cies in making decisions. These are aspects of learning that
> cannot be handled as subject matter in the classroom but
> which represent individual learnings in which the sensitive
> reactions of the counselor are necessary to maximize each
> student's development. The new emphasis in counseling
> will be on helping individuals to develop individuality, per-
> sonally discovered value systems, and skills in making
> personal judgments in a somewhat chaotic world.

Frequently used by the counselor-educators are such terms
as "decision-making," "self-understanding," "self-discovery," and
"self-identification." One raised the issue clearly when he stated:
"The paramount question around which counseling will be
structured will be 'who am I?' and not 'what shall I do for a
living?' "

2. *Self-understanding cannot be in isolation from the conditions of the culture in which the student lives.* The needs of
society and their impact upon the student's choice are clearly
stressed by a number of the educators. Some go so far as to
suggest that the future will see less emphasis upon the good
of the individual but more upon the general good of society as
a whole. Others would be deeply concerned that individual
self-realization not be subordinated to the current needs of
society. A thread of concern runs through many reactions
regarding the dangers involved in individuals being seen as
means to an end, the end being social good.

There is a confusion here which is often not resolved, not in
this report or elsewhere. The fallacy arises from placing the
individual in opposition to society, making it a matter of the
individual *versus* society, "versus" rather than "and." Social
need and individual need are often fused, not separated. A
society is *composed of* men, and a man finds his individual satisfaction *in* society. The counselor must be highly conscious of

the "and" and constantly recall that both counselor and client live in society, draw from it, give to it, are inseparable from it. "Society" must not be confused with the political entity known as the State.

3. That emphasis be given to the importance of a *more effective and psychologically meaningful assistance in the making of educational-vocational plans.* A few believe that this function will decrease in significance, but the majority believe that it will increase but with a different emphasis. The basic task generally seen is that of helping the individual understand himself in the process of seeing the relationship of his talents to the educational opportunities and vocational needs of his society. This then becomes a self-understanding of a general sort with applications to educational and vocational future rather than vocational choice as an end in itself.

4. Comparatively little attention is given to the process of *psychological appraisal as it is affected by the use of tests.* This may be either because the use of psychometrics in self-finding is taken for granted as a necessary and legitimate means to an end or because they think tests are used overmuch.[1]

5. A good many comments are suggestive of the *need of the counselor to study cultural and occupational changes as these may affect the general development of the student* as well as his educational and vocational planning. The rapid changes anticipated are taken into account by several who believe that counselors should assist students in developing greater adaptability and "the ability to live in a world of insecurity in which one is always adjusting and never adjusted."

6. Another major emphasis of counselor-educators is *the contribution of the counselor to teaching staff, administrators, and parents.* Here the focus is upon a respectable fraction of a counselor's time being spent in consultation with teachers, counseling with them, contributing to their better understanding of student characteristics and the meeting of normal classroom problems which involve pupil-teacher relationships. The counselor is to serve as a resource person on human development for the school principal and for parents.

What is now being done fairly extensively in the elementary school in the form of frequent parent conferences and a feeling of responsibility for helping the parent understand his own child is seen also as a developing function for the high school counselor. The broad area of interpretation of student behavior to

---

[1] It may be a combination of the two for it is too often assumed that *of course* tests are used in every counseling relationship. Not so, nor should they be used as a crutch by the counselor who doesn't know what else to do.

other adults is seen as a second major focus for the high school counselor as well.

7. Several educators believe that *the counselor must enter more actively into curriculum development* in terms of his knowledge of changing student characteristics and needs.

Other areas touched upon by some of the educators:

a. More contact of the high school counselor with elementary school counselors and elementary school children, and more attention given to counseling in the elementary school.

b. Coordination of the resources of the school with the resources of the community because some of the needs now being met by the school could be met by community agencies.

c. The counselor as an individual who serves as the hub of a pupil service team, the one who coordinates the work of the other personnel who provide services to students outside of the classroom.

One imaginative counselor-educator, after describing the marked social and technological changes that he believes will affect the schools of the next decade or two, describes the basic activities of the counselor in 1980 as follows:

> Information about the pupil and the consequence of his alternatives will be available upon a push of a button in 1980. In addition it will be possible to characterize the pupil and project him by machine into a number of different perspectives. [IBM says this can be done now as far as the computer is concerned.] The counselor's activities, therefore, will be focused not only upon the pupil's comprehension of the information about himself but, more importantly, upon bringing the student to comprehend the relationship of self and the world in which he is engaged. . . .
>
> In 1980 the activities upon which the identity of the counselor will be validated are, in order of importance: (1) his counseling; (2) his advising of teachers; (3) his revision of programs of education; (4) his programming and use of machines that convey the information that he seeks.

## Emerging Perceptions of the Counselor's Relation to Students

A merging of the responses of counselors and counselor-educators with a very considerable body of literature on new conceptions in counseling makes it possible to list what appears to be the directions in which counseling will be moving in the near future. The functions projected here *relate only to the counselor's work with students*. His part in the total school program is considered in the next chapter.

## 1. *To Contribute to Student Self-Understanding and Self-Acceptance*

One major task of a counselor in his relationship to the student is that he contributes to a growing maturity of self-understanding. This means that the realities of his personal characteristics and aspirations are seen by the student in their relationships to cultural changes and educational and vocational opportunities. This does not sound too new, but the flavor is different because the stress is upon giving attention to counseling as a *prevention* rather than as a cure, counseling which stresses *growth, self-determination,* and *self-responsibility.* This is a remedy for the "man in the white coat" emphasis whereby the counselor takes over and attempts to cure the ills of the student. Counseling has become a way of assisting at different choice points in the life of the growing child and youth, *assisting him in the art and science of making informed decisions.* The movement is from self-perceptions and awarenesses outward rather than focusing upon information that is outside the student's awareness and concern.

It is not an easy task for any individual to disclose enough of himself so as to enable others to contribute their insights to his own growing understanding. Much advice is given to the growing child and student but unless it is given under certain conditions very little of it is effective. There is some evidence to suggest that, no matter how excellent the advice and information, unless it is related to *the student's desire to know,* unless it is focused upon those personal concerns that have immediate meaning for him, the advice is forgotten or at least perceived in a distorted form.

Our very culture does not make it easy for the individual to engage in this process of psychological sharing with another. Studies of young people make it clear that adolescents want so badly to be accepted and liked by other people that they frequently value other people's opinions above their own. They attempt, in a sense, to become what others want them to be. Under these conditions it is difficult for a student to disclose what he feels and thinks about himself for fear of being rejected or disliked. Unless there is opportunity for an individual to establish a close relationship with at least one other human being, a relationship which is nonthreatening, it is easy for a conflict to develop between what he senses himself to be and what he would like to be in response to others' demands.

Counseling, then, focuses upon self-understanding but interpreted in terms of a concern for personality development which includes the acquisition of knowledge, its integration, and its application to decisions about life roles. He is concerned with a student's "problems" but is likely to see a problem as a normal developmental task to be considered within the range of tasks for that student's stage of development. The counselor is concerned more with a student's need for defining his roles in school, community, vocation, and marriage than with personality reconstruction. He may well have to be concerned with what Perry calls an intrapersonal conflict and he should be equipped to recognize the nature of such a state of internal confusion. But this is only a necessary correlate of the counselor's major responsibility, that of contributing to a student's growing self-understanding so that he, the student, can cope better with his growth conflicts and can clarify his social roles.

## 2. To Be Sensitive to Cultural Changes Which Affect Student Self-Understanding

What the student knows about himself must be related to the changing world around him. One function of counseling is to assist the student to find the several environments — educational, social, vocational — in which he can become the most completely involved and gain the greatest sense of self-fulfillment. The counselor must be sensitive, not only to the student's characteristics, but to the characterstics of our culture which will mean most to the student. The dynamics of our society must be as meaningful to the counselor as the dynamics of the student.

The counselor's task is to assist the student in the decisions to be made regarding the educational, vocational, and social environments which he will find most satisfying and in which he can become most productive. Also, perhaps, to be aware of those characteristics of our society with which this student will be in conflict. The counselor is a person whose richness of understanding of the changing world should match his depth of understanding of the individual with whom he is working.

## 3. To Help Students to Make Informed Educational and Vocational Choices

The choice of a career field is a traditional function of the counselor, but here again, the approach suggested is different from the traditional one. The start is from the *student's perceptions of himself* and of the kinds of needs these perceptions reflect, rather than from the vocational demands as such. The basis of choice rests upon whatever factors have the most significance for the person making the choice. It is now believed that choices made regarding a vocation are an attempt upon the part of the individual to find a vocational environment which will contribute to the kind of person he wishes to become. In other words, it starts from his perception of himself, both as he is and as he wishes to be.

The vocational counseling suggested is nontraditional in a second sense. The choices to be made are several, not one, hopefully each one in the sequence utilizing more information about the vocational world and about oneself. Perhaps one's vocational choice is never completed — any one choice is an event in a lifelong process. The student faces a real world in which he must be economically self-supporting. It is also a world in which he attempts to find increasingly satisfying ways of living a life as well as making a living.

Although for most students educational and vocational career choices are inseparable it is less true for students who are academically gifted. Students who are capable of undertaking work that will lead them to college and possibly to graduate school impose a handicap upon themselves if they make their vocational choice too early, at least if it is a choice of a specific nature. Preferences falling within a broad area of activity such as the sciences, business, the arts, human relations, still leave the student much leeway to make choices of an increasingly specific nature from time to time throughout his college program. Although vocational motivation is not to be underestimated for the academically capable student it should not be a limiting factor. The emphasis for such a student should be upon choices which contribute to the greatest possible intellectual growth and the satisfying of intellectual curiosities. Dr. John Gardner has stated it well:

> The superior student . . . should be encouraged to develop his intellectual talents on as broad a front as possible. . . . Under no circumstances should he be urged to make early vocational choices which eliminate some of these intellectual potentialities at the expense of others. . . . We must avoid a cut and dried vocationalism which urges the youngster toward premature "practical decisions," and puts him too early on a specialized path when he might have developed more broadly.

Youth must be prepared for the inevitability of rapid change and be assisted in developing enough flexibility to meet these changes. Vocational planning should include the very real possibility that the vocation chosen may change materially within the next 10 years. Both the student's thinking about the vocation and his preparation for it should involve an allowance for this kind of change. Helping youth to accept the fact that they will continue to live in a world of insecurity and tension is a significant counseling goal. The "adjusted" person is an anomaly and perhaps a bore as well, but one who accepts as inevitable the need for constant adjustment to change becomes a delight. He is also more likely to be perceived as a mature person.

The counselor is a talent-hunter in cooperation with the student. He seeks to help the student find the way in which he can be unique. And each person wants a sense of uniqueness. The talents sought for may have strong vocational implications but the more basic matter is the recognition of the talent itself. This is true self-discovery, the finding of the talent that may otherwise be buried. Or the talent that the *student* has buried out of a sense of its being unwanted. Talent hunting is a basic form of vocational counseling.

## 4. *To Develop Group Learning Experiences for Students*

Although both counselors and counselor-educators in the Commission Studies had little to say about group guidance, it seems clear that the counselor must accept responsibility for using wisely what might better be called "planned group experiences." It is doubtful that what is presently called group guidance can be justified on the basis of saving time for the counselor. What should be considered is that some of the outcomes to be expected from individual counseling are different from those sought for in group experience. It is clear that the counselor should see counseling and planned group experiences as having different values for the student. They are both tools for him to utilize in his attempt to assist the student toward better self-understanding and wiser decision-making. Hospitals and medical clinics have used group psychotherapy for some time. Schools, on the other hand, have used group guidance classes most frequently for instructional purposes. Somewhere in between is the counselor's use of the group experience in which group interaction and learning from others under skilled leadership becomes valuable for students who are not in need of psychotherapy.

In elementary school or in high school, it is possible for both counselor and remedial teacher to work together with groups needing some type of remedial assistance, each contributing his own particular skills to the development of the group. In one school, for example, the remedial teacher and the counselor handle the same group on alternate days, one working with the skills needed and the other working with individual pupil attitudes toward the subject and the general reasons for achievement and nonachievement in the development of skills.

Group experiences may be utilized by the counselor to orient the student in certain kinds of understandings that will make individual counseling more valuable to him. Beyond this, however, is the opportunity for the student to learn from other students and to see himself reflected in their reactions to him. This is a value not to be found by any other procedure. Leadership in such a group experience calls for an understanding of the dynamics of group interaction that makes it quite different

130

from the supervision of homeroom situations or occupational information classes.

## 5. *To Increase Student Self-Reliance*

There is general agreement that it is not the counselor's task to change the person but to clarify the student's understandings of himself and of the resources available to him. It becomes a task of *assisting a student to learn how to make decisions*, rather than the counselor's assuming responsibility for the decisions that must be made. It is a task, furthermore, which will stress the need for a student at any level to try out his own perceptions of himself in situations that will test the validity of the assumptions that he makes about himself.

Counselors have no business making things easy for a student. Rather, their task is to give the student enough insight and courage so that he may try the hard things for himself. This may mean learning from mistakes but someone has to give the student the courage to make the mistake in order to learn from it. If the counselor's relationship to the student makes him more dependent, then the counselor has failed. There are times, of course, when the counselor must give support in a time of crisis even though no decision is made and no solution is found. It is more important, however, that the counselor assist the student to become an increasingly self-understanding and self-reliant individual, and that the counselor work to the same end with other adults who influence the student.

In a study carried on in the Plumas Unified School District in California, academically talented students were given opportunities to engage in both counseling and group sessions with the counselor. As a result of the combination of this experience during the summer of 1959, one student reported that he was "suddenly given all sorts of responsibilities. Now it is up to me to figure out my life plans and what I could do best. I felt for the first time that it was my sole responsibility, not my parents' and not the school's. . . ."

## 6. *To Counsel Girls Realistically*

Many changes are likely to take place within the next decade or two that will modify the role of women in our culture. In fact, many changed conditions are present that are poorly recognized by parents and educators. It is quite clear that the sheltered, submissive, and dependent female of the Victorian days of our society is a thing of the past. Marriage is seen as a working partnership, and it can be an effective and constructive state of existence only if the relationship is accepted by both parties without the interference of inadequate stereotypes of either male or female. This partnership is essential since both husband and wife at some periods in their life are likely to be out of the home at the same time. Responsibility for the home and children must be shared between husband and wife, without clinging to the older concept of the husband as breadwinner only and wife as homemaker only.

If it is recalled that at least nine out of every ten women are likely to work outside the home during the course of their lives, and that six out of every ten women now working are now married, the relationship of vocational planning to marriage planning is a reality that must be accepted and given careful thought by the counselor. Increasingly women are entering or re-entering the labor force in their mid-thirties, and many girls will work immediately after leaving school. Vocational planning is as essential for them as it is for boys. With the increasing importance of women in the labor force, the increasing need of society for their talents in the various vocations, and the increasing need of women to find additional self-respect and self-confidence in some activity outside the home, it is important that more women be encouraged to engage in education beyond high school. It is also desirable that more qualified college women be encouraged to take graduate work.

The vocational counseling of girls involves the necessity of facing what will be for many of them a dual role — that of wife, homemaker, and mother, and that of worker for some major part of her life in an occupation outside the home. The girl who marries and later works not only has two lives, a life in the home and a life in a job, but she has two relationships with her husband. This calls for a kind of marriage reality for which girls may be partially prepared before marriage. As the marriage-plus-job relationship develops, it calls also for additional counseling assistance to young adults.

7. *To Accept and Encourage Diversity in Talents*

It has always been the counselor's responsibility to be aware of individual differences, but the new awareness calls for recognition of an increasing variety of talents that are needed by society — intellectual, social, mechanical, and artistic. Counselors carry a heavier responsibility than ever for knowing how to identify many kinds of human talent and how to interpret their significance to the student possessing them. The counselor must himself be respectful of talents different from those he possesses if he is to deal fairly with them. There is a tendency to be threatened by that which someone else possesses and we do not possess. This is fatal in the counseling relationship.

Beyond this the counselor must be dedicated to the free choice of an individual to use his talents in ways that seem justifiable to him. After the counselor has contributed as much as he can to the student's self-understanding and to his awareness of the culture in which he lives, the moral justification of a student's use of his talents is his own, not the counselor's.

## What Counselors Look Like as People

From an informal survey of school counselors in metropolitan New York, made by the International Research Associates for the Ford Fund for the Advancement of Education, we have these charming vignettes of city-school counselors:

> 1. She is a Negro woman, in her early fifties, short, warm, big bosomy. She is one of the most charming, intelligent people I've ever met. She seems to be a real expert in her field, very articulate, with wide interests and tremendous enthusiasms. It seems that helping people and loving them is her great job. She is a most alive human being.

(In this case, she is a widow without children, working in a depressed-area school — she had to look up the records to recall her salary. She has an M.A., reads a lot, and is active in community organizations.)

> 2. Mr. G. is a tall, youthful-looking man possessing a pleasant countenance. He is a friendly, relaxed person . . . was very patient throughout the interview, and upon its completion told another counselor that he had found the interview fruitful . . . I felt that Mr. G. possessed considerable tact, humility and patience.

(Mr. G. is 50 years old; he works in a city public school, has an A.B., is married, has two sons. His wife, also with an A.B., teaches. His hobbies are: "listening to music, reading, fishing, painting, woodcraft, talking.")

> 3. Mrs. D. is a pleasant-looking, gray-haired woman — tall. She is a relaxed person and relates easily, is unaffected and relatively free in expressing herself. She seems to have a wonderful understanding of teen-age problems, without being overimpressed with her role as a counselor. She seems capable of always taking things in her stride.

(This 55-year-old woman is married, with three girls and a boy. Her husband teaches but in a different school. Their outside activities are very limited.)

> 4. She is a short, dark-haired, pleasant-faced woman. She has a ready smile and is warm, friendly and humorous.

(She is 42 years old, the mother of two little girls of nine and twelve, has an M.A. and a Ph.D., was born in New York City, works in a middle- and upper-class suburb for $7,500 per year and the pleasure of it. She has lived a year in France and traveled elsewhere.)

These four counselors are in no sense representative of all school counselors. They come in all sizes and ages and all patterns of personality. These four are real people, however, not stylized images. They possess some of the qualities that seem desirable in counselors — intelligence, cultural awareness, broad tolerance and patience, a sense of humor and of the fitness of things. They are comfortable people without in any sense being passive and complacent. They like children but do not lose their heads over them. They would be good companions on a long trip.

The image of the counselor presented thus far is that of a person who is increasingly aware of his specialized responsibilities. He is a person with a mission, the boundaries of which are encompassable. He is an educator and he is a psychologist but neither term describes his work with adequate preciseness. He is a specialist in student behavior, its present manifestations and its potentials for growth. He sees the student as a dynamic changing personality, constantly affected by various environments, each of which in turn is dynamic and moving in certain directions. He is a specialist in human relations and in the psychology and sociology that makes people behave the way they do.

The image here presented is that of a *changing counselor*, too. The look is to the future; each counselor will move from where he is now in the direction of these stated goals if the needs of our changing children and youth are to be met. He may never arrive there — he may find it quite enough to keep moving. No one expects any more. No counselor need be a superman but he must be a person who is able to live with the awareness that he can never quite live up to his job. All who want a placid self-contained life should apply elsewhere.

# *The Changing Guidance Program and the Counselor*

# The Changing Guidance Program and the Counselor

## CONTENTS

## It Is Recommended:

1. That national, state, and local school boards and other agencies consider the development of highly competent school counseling services an area of critical need in view of the necessity for children and youth to adapt readily to the changing scientific, technological, and social cultures which affect their personal lives and the life of the nation.

2. That the professional job description of a school counselor specify that he perform four major functions: (a) counsel with students; (b) consult with teachers, administrators, and parents as they in turn deal with students; (c) study the changing facts about the student population and interpret what is found to school committees and administrators; (d) coordinate counseling resources in school and between school and community. From two-thirds to three-fourths of the counselor's time, in either elementary or high school, should be committed to the first two of these functions. Activities that do not fall into one of these four areas neither should be expected nor encouraged as part of the counselor's regular working schedule.

3. That a local school administration is justified in stating that it has a counseling program only when the school has qualified counselors in sufficient number to meet the needs for counseling of all students. An instructional program assumes qualified teachers in sufficient number to meet instructional needs, and a counseling program must be defined by similar criteria. The ratio of counselors to students (counseling load) is determined by the educational and developmental needs of students and the adequacy of the total school program to meet these needs. A ratio of the general magnitude of one full-time qualified counselor to each 300 high school students, with the ratio of students to counselor somewhat higher in the elementary school, is proposed as a reasonable expectation if the counselor is to discharge the four functions defined in Recommendation 2 of this chapter.

4. That the pupil personnel program of a school be defined as that combination of services rendered by a team of pupil personnel specialists — school counselor, school psychologist, school social worker, school health officer, and school attendance worker. These specialists work in close relationship to teachers and administrators and are of service to them as they are to students and parents.

5. That pupil personnel services rendered by school counselors, school psychologists, school social workers, and related specialists be accepted as an essential part of the school program, as essential as instruction and administration, and that the minimal budget allocated to such services be somewhere within the range of five to eight per cent of the total budget of the school or school system.

6. That the school board employ counselors who are first of all technically competent and sensitive to others but, all other things being equal, they employ the counselor who is the more widely read, the more traveled, and the more culturally mature.

7. That school boards and school administrators be increasingly attentive to the quality of the individuals they select to serve as counselors and be willing to compensate the better qualified counselors accordingly.

8. That adequate clerical help, or dictating equipment plus clerical help, be provided by school boards so that excessive clerical responsibilities do not vitiate the counselor's major functions.

9. That counseling in the elementary school be considered vital to the welfare of both the children and the nation, but that continuing study be made of this function since the actual course of counseling development in the elementary school has not yet been charted. In the elementary school the identification of talents and of early patterns of development is the joint responsibility of teacher, counselor, and other pupil personnel specialists. The responsibility of the counselor for identification is clear, but the relationships between these personnel overlap to a greater degree than in the secondary school. Clearly, also it is the responsibility of the counselor to provide realistic social and vocational orientation in the elementary school, particularly for the students who terminate their formal education at this level. To be kept in mind, however, is the conclusion from recent studies that students in the junior high school and earlier are often psychologically unready to make a reasoned vocational choice although they may profit from vocational discussion and exploration.

## CHAPTER 6

# The Changing Guidance Program and the Counselor

THE RECENT HISTORY of American secondary education suggests that the guidance program has been designed to complement in certain ways the total school program. More bluntly, the guidance function has met some of the deficiencies of the school program and has "taken up the slack" where need existed. This accounts for the jerry-built appearance of the guidance program in many schools.

In 1951 the U. S. Office of Education convened a conference to provide a blueprint for pupil personnel services in elementary and secondary schools. The conference proposed that: (a) there were nine distinctive pupil personnel (or guidance) services — *child accounting and attendance, orientation, counseling services, clinical services, individual analysis, health services, home-community-school services, occupational and educational information services,* and *placement and follow-up services;* (b) related to pupil personnel services, but often involving other school personnel, were the handling of disciplinary problems, financial aid, and remedial services; (c) considered to be a part of the curricular program of the school were student activities, group activities, and special education.

During the past decade some of these nine personnel functions have become a part of the total administrative and curricular program of the school. In 1959, Frank L. Sievers of the U. S. Office of Education, in discussing the administration of the National Defense Education Act, epitomized the school guidance program as consisting of six elements: *analysis, information, orientation, counseling, placement, follow-up.* This is a marked paring down of the 1951 statement, and it is to be anticipated that more of the student needs formerly met by pupil personnel services will be seen as a responsibility of the administrative and teaching staff. The only reason that the orientation of new students, pupil accounting, home and community relations, and educational and occupational information should be considered pupil personnel services is that no other agency in the school considers itself responsible for them. Yet all are schoolwide functions for which school administrators and the teaching staff have major concern. This is equally true for discipline (affecting administrator and teacher) and remedial work (affecting teachers in their respective subject fields).

The changes taking place in school plant, organization, curriculum, and instructional activities will enable the school as a whole to achieve educational aims hitherto considered the primary responsibility of the guidance program. Much of the "student personnel point of view" will be integrated into the general school program of the future. Such matters as the identification and development of student talent, the relating of the intellectual emphasis to vocational and citizenship preparation, the effective transition in and out of a given school unit, the encouragement of individual diversity and of creativity in thinking are not tasks for one segment of the school program but are parts of the total school effort. Dean John L. Fisher has said:

> At its best a school guidance service increases the efficiency of everything else that happens in the school because it facilitates both understanding by pupils and parents of what the school has to offer. Such a service helps everyone to make wiser decisions about using what is available. The dollars spent on such services can assure much greater returns on the vastly bigger sums spent to support the total instructional program. The lack of an effective guidance program often means that the costs of providing an expensive educational opportunity for pupils may be almost completely wasted.

## The School Counselor

There is currently a great deal of confusion over the terms "guidance," "counseling," and "counselor." The objectives of the guidance *program* may be manifold and with varied *functions* such as counseling included in the program, but often the only *person* involved is the school counselor. This is particularly true in smaller schools, whether elementary or secondary, and these are in the majority. In smaller schools "the counselor" is the sole student personnel worker, and he is spread very thin indeed. Whatever is done in the way of administering a program of psychological measurement, orientation, personal records, educational and occupational information, sometimes home relations and discipline, is done by the counselor *in addition to* counseling.

Actually, of course, there is usually too little time for counseling with students or consulting with teachers and parents. Counselors are pulled away from their counselor function in two ways: (a) in performing guidance program functions other than counseling; and (b) in doing clerical work, serving as advisers to clubs, assemblies, and social events, substituting for absent teachers, and engaging in similar nonguidance activities.

Earlier it was stated that if the school is to fulfill its major function of providing for the intellectual, social, and vocational competencies of its students — and, in particular, to fulfill its task of stimulating and facilitating intellectual growth — it must release to other community agencies some of the functions it is now performing. Likewise if the counselor is to do what he is held most responsible for, some of what is now part of the guidance program must be absorbed either within the school itself or by other agencies in the community. Vocational placement, as an example, should be conceived of as a responsibility of state and community if the counselor and other school staff are to be left free to engage in educational placement, a task which only they can perform. Many State Employment Services currently consider themselves responsibile for the vocational placement of entry workers. This is done, of course, with assistance and cooperation from the school. But the primary responsibility rests with the employment service, not the school.

## The Counselor's Program Responsibilities

A distinction exists between performing a function directly and seeing that it is done. It is proposed that the counselor is responsible directly for:

a. *counseling with students* on matters of self-understanding, decision-making, and planning, using both the interview and group situations;

b. *consulting with staff and parents* on questions of student understanding and student management;

c. *studying changes in the character of the student population* and making a continuing interpretation of this information to the school administration and to curriculum-development committees;

d. *performing a liaison function* between other school and community counseling resources and facilitating their use by teachers and students.

Beyond these four functions the counselor may well want to get things done, but he cannot do them himself and discharge his primary obligations. In the past if the counselor suggested that something additional needed to be done, he was promptly assigned the performance of the function that he suggested. It is by this route that he became the teacher of occupational information classes, the director of the orientation program for new students, the provider of vocational placement

141

services, and the like. Before the advent of the school psychologist and the school social worker, the counselor also made whatever diagnostic study was made of difficult student situations and visited the home or consulted with the teacher about home conditions.

A 1960 publication of the Council of Chief State School Officers entitled *Responsibilites of the State Departments of Education for Pupil Personnel Services* lists five student personnel services — attendance, guidance, school health, school psychological work, and school social work. At one time all of these were considered part of the guidance program and, of course, in some situations this is still true. What is spoken of as "guidance services" in this publication is far more focused in nature than it would have been a decade ago, although it still includes providing educational-occupational information to pupils, parents, and teachers, and providing vocational placement services for students.

On the other hand, no mention is made in the publication cited of the contribution of the counselor to teacher and administrator, to curriculum development, and to the provision of needed changes in the school environment. The terminology used in this publication is still a confusing one of "guidance and counseling programs" in which it is stated that "the school counselor functions in such essential activities of the guidance program as . . ." and then lists the various elements of the guidance program! It is apparent that there is little in the way of guidance program except for the functions performed by the counselor. And a "counselor" is seen as a "guidance worker."

The Commission on Guidance in American Schools proposes that the confusing term "guidance services" be abandoned — and that pupil personnel services be seen as the activities of the school counselor, the school psychologist, the school social worker, the school health officer, and the school attendance officer. Pupil personnel services thus become broader than any so-called guidance services and yet a central function of such services is the work of the school counselor. His work with students, staff, and parents is clear. In addition, he must be enough of an educational statesman to see that provision is made for the kind of information that students must have to make wise and informed decisions and to become well informed about themselves; that there is provision for adequate orientation experiences in the early days of the students' life at school; that there is liaison with city or state vocational placement agencies, health, welfare, and recreation agencies, etc.

This concept of the counselor as a member of a team of pupil personnel workers does not mean that the concept of guidance is abandoned. It merely means that the diffused concept of a guidance program be simplified. What is commonly called guidance is a *philosophy*, a point of view with regard to the individualization of the student's educational experience; part of this, the coordination of his personal learning in and out of the classroom to the end of better personal understanding and wiser judgment and decision-making is a particular responsibility of the counselor. He will assist some students directly. Others will grow toward effective maturity with a minimum of counselor help or with only the basic help of parents and teachers. But what he does is only one way of carrying a philosophy of guidance into action. Teachers and administrators also have major responsibility for this point of view.

### The Counselor as Specialist

The description of the counselor by some as a generalist and by others as a specialist provides for further confusion in thinking. If the statement of terms is clear, he can be seen as both. (a) The counselor is a generalist in the sense of his being widely available to the total school population and attempting to possess some knowledge of the total school program. He is a generalist also in the sense that he should be acquainted with the complete scope of school referral resources and know how these may be utilized by himself or by other members of the staff. (b) The counselor is a specialist in his specific knowledge of the student and in his ability to relate himself effectively to the student in both individual and group situations. He is a specialist in the total scope of student learnings in and out of the classroom. He is a specialist in the collation and interpretation of information about individual students and student populations — to the student himself, to staff, to administrators, and to parents.

In the decades ahead the counselor will share some specialized functions with others, but he must not lose his distinctive ability to see the whole — the whole school, the whole range of students, the whole student.

The function of the other pupil personnel specialists seem fairly clear by the nature of the terminology used. Certainly, there can be little question about the normal duties of the attendance officer and the doctor or nurse responsible for the school health service. Similarly, the work of the school social worker is clearly that of casework with students and families in an attempt to remove obstacles to the student's optimally profiting from the school experience. The work of the school pyschologist is somewhat less clear. Formerly his function has been that of a psychological diagnostician and therapist working with so-called problem cases that are complex in nature and require intensive attention. He may work with the pupil directly or with the pupil and the teacher in a clinical type of service involving a relatively small but rather critical number of pupils within a school population. A more recent perception of the school psychologist is that he also provides broader services to the school staff as a specialist on learning problems and psychological conditions that affect the classroom learning experience.

Clearly, if both school psychologist and school counselor are on a staff, the respective functions of each will have to be carefully delineated to prevent undesirable overlap. It is more likely that the average staff will contain a larger number of school counselors than school psychologists and that the latter will perform the somewhat more specialized functions suggested above. Each is equipped to carry out to some degree many of the functions performed by the other.

It seems quite likely that the counselor's rather large responsibility for understanding psychological appraisal, as well as the various kinds of constantly changing information needed for student planning and transition to the next educational level, will require specialization within a group of counselors in any given school. As a given school employs more counselors, there will be a natural tendency for some counselors to shift to more intensive operation in certain areas of counseling or to become especially well informed on certain kinds of information. As a result, other counselors will come to depend on a particular counselor for certain kinds of information or services. Some of this division of labor could certainly be planned.

Steps could be taken to see that some counselors are encouraged to become the best informed of all on further educational opportunities, while still others attempt to keep up to date regarding changing occupational conditions and demands. Another might become apt in the interpretation of school population information to teaching staff and administration. Another specialization might involve the school's liaison with community agencies. All must remain specialists in student understanding and have the capacity to develop a counseling relationship with students and a consulting relationship with teachers and parents. In any case, *there should be no regression to the counselor's serving as a general agent for school functions not performed by anyone else.* The use of valuable counselor time to administer and score tests, for example, is one of the most wasteful phenomena of the past two or three decades.

*Information Centers*

The manner in which psychological and sociological information is supplied is responsive to technological advances. So

144

let us project a little into the future. The school system of the near future will have information centers where three kinds of information are electronically collated, analyzed, and transmitted for use by various members of the staff — centers for educational information, for vocational information, and for information about student characteristics. These centers will keep such information up to date and automatically transmit it to each school for use by teachers and various pupil personnel workers. There is urgent need to correct the current situation in many schools, where educational and vocational information is out of date and is not only worthless but dangerous to use.

The center for information on student characteristics, for example, should have computers which can be fed a pattern of student characteristics in order to yield a number of educational or vocational alternatives, each with appropriate degree of risk or margin of error. The computers can be used for such work during nights and weekends, when they are not involved in routine duties. A counselor with prior knowledge that a student wanted to see him about educational or vocational planning could, the night before, punch in the data on this student and find from the computer's calculations the most likely prospects for the student, whether it be college to be attended, curriculum to be chosen, or vocational field.

In all of this, of course, the choice is to remain with the student. The counselor uses the computer merely to make available to the student a more precise list of probabilities. It could be a more complete list too, since the searching process of the computer might bring into focus probabilities which would not have occurred to the counselor within the short course of the interview.

*Research in the Personnel Program*

Research in the program of pupil personnel services is an essential, and the school counselor and school psychologist may well be expected to lead in developing useful approaches. Henry S. Dyer of the Educational Testing Service has suggested a number of kinds of research in which counselors might well engage. He believes that one of the most urgent areas of need concerns the relative effectiveness of the various kinds of communications that are used in school and college personnel programs. He is appalled that many widely used communications have never been subjected to research verification as to effectiveness. Such simple things as a description of a school curriculum or the interpretation of academic progress may sound quite confusing to parent or student. Research is needed on the *form of communication* that will most accurately present the information to be transmitted. Information in a school or college bulletin may be badly misinterpreted without check as to the validity of the perception developed by the reader.

Dyer speaks also of such simple but useful research as information contributing to better identification of students who may be "trouble-prone." The counselor might make a collection of case histories of students with notable social or academic difficulties. By comparing these histories point by point with students whose adjustment and achievement is adequate, the counselor might arrive at some body of fairly well defined characteristics that would serve as warning signals to teachers and counselors in that school.

More basic is the responsibility of the counselor mentioned earlier for studying information about the changing character of the student population and securing some understanding of the changing conditions of the community and their impact upon student population. In a school system the information should be provided by a research director with the counselor responsible for seeing that this information is utilized in his own work with students and is interpreted for the use of the rest of the school staff. Lacking a research director, the counselor must assume responsibility for seeing that the information is secured.

The idea of research frightens some counselors, also teachers and school administrators. They conjure up images of experimental research — manipulation or measurement of one factor in a situation while holding other variables constant — or an analysis of data which requires the use of statistical formulae containing strange symbols. Such research will be engaged in by few school counselors — those who are equipped should certainly be encouraged to do so — but many *service studies* need to be made. Descriptive data about students, about the situations in which students operate, and about the factors operating in the process of counseling are a first step and can be collected by anyone. Care must be used in drawing inferences from such data but the counselor can seek help on this technical point. *Curiosity* is a first requisite, followed by *accuracy* in collecting information and *care* in making inferences from the information. More mistakes can be made by counselors who assume that they know but never attempt to find out than by counselors who conduct studies but do so poorly.

## Unrealistic Emphases for the Counselor

What is said about conducting simple investigations as an appropriate task for the counselor should be contrasted with some of the impossible expectations held for the counselor. A counselor is often expected to act in some mysterious way to get a student to conform to the school program, whether or not conformity is the best course of action for this particular student. Sometimes he is expected to effect marked changes in a student's personality.

1. Counselor responsibility for the disciplinary functions of a school should be clarified. Except in rare cases, counselors cannot maintain effective counseling relationships with students in general and at the same time be responsible for *disciplinary action* with a few. For the counselor to work with a student who is in difficulty is a natural expectation for a person who is presumed to be aware of pupil behavior and of possible reasons for it. This is quite different from making the counselor the school's disciplinary officer or even an adjunct to action that needs to be taken.

Counselors, and teachers, cannot expect to remain aloof from behavior problems which get students into trouble. But each must serve in his role as counselor or teacher. Following the lead of some universities, a school might even appoint a specially designated counselor to work *as a counselor* with students who have exhibited rebellious and nonsocial behavior. This counselor may be accepted *only* as a specialized person and students generally are not likely to seek him out. But he may serve a very constructive purpose. If the student can secure insight into the reasons for his behavior and can accept greater responsibility for his behavior, no action may be necessary. If action is necessary, for the protection of the school or some segment of the school population, this is administrative action in which the counselor should have no part. To specialize in psychological rehabilitation is appropriate for a counselor, but it is not appropriate for him to act as an administrative officer of the school.

2. Frequently the counselor is expected to stimulate a chronic underachiever to some more seemingly appropriate standard of performance. Some of the research recently developed regarding the attitude of the student who persistently performs at a level below what is presumed to be his potential suggests that the situation is far more complex than formerly perceived. When counselors are asked to counsel all underachievers and "do something about them," they have been asked to deal with a condition which may be part of the basic personality structure of the students involved. Chronic underachievement appears to have strong overtones of social hostility towards school and towards authority in general. The pattern may have had its origin in the fourth or fifth grade. No amount of stimulation or persuasion is likely to meet this personality condition.

It is true that the counselor might discover that a given underachiever is highly creative in directions hitherto unknown to him and such self-discovery might provide him with a self-perception more appropriate to intellectual growth. The counselor may also discover some of the psychological bases of a student's underachievment, perhaps emotional rather than intellectual in nature, and help the teacher to understand a little better how to deal with the student's needs. In general, however, the assumption that counselors should work with all students who are in social or academic difficulty is a costly and ineffective use of their time. The counselor's capacity for assisting students may be much better utilized when normal developmental needs and assistance in decision-making are considered his major responsibility.

## Special Emphases for Pupil Personnel Services in the Elementary School

A group of consultants to the Secretary of Health, Education and Welfare in recommending (fall, 1960) that the National Defense Education Act be extended to the elementary school made this statement: "The elementary schools contain a much larger pool of talent, in proportion to the size of the age group in the total population, than is found elsewhere in this educational system. . . . It should be emphasized that the guidance effort must be developed in appropriate ways in the elementary school for the earlier identification and development of talent."

The quotation epitomizes the new look in the elementary school pupil personnel work. This is an emphasis upon the positive rather than upon the negative, upon the identification of pupil characteristics and talents, upon the developmental needs of all pupils rather than deviate and problem students only. The elementary school child early needs some appreciation of who he is and of what he is capable of doing. Unless this is accomplished, the motivation for making the fullest use of himself will die a-borning in many lives. It is in the elementary school that we have the early beginning of attitudes towards school and towards self which result in either steady growth or in an attitude of resentment and hostility which results in underachievement and early dropout. It is in the elementary school that the important transition from home to school is made, one of the most difficult of the transitions in the child's school history.

The critical question is whether or not the elementary school will learn from the experience of the secondary school and build a counseling program which is not crisis-oriented. Beyond this, there are a number of specific differences between the elementary school and the secondary school.

Because of the relationship between parent and child and between teacher and child, the counselor must work much more

148

in a team approach with both parent and teacher than is essential or even desirable at the secondary school level. The elementary school child is a relatively dependent member of the home, and the home is a major influence in his life. Because of these conditions there is need for the counselor to work closely with the teacher, the school social worker (if such exists in the system), and the parent in planning for changes in the home that will make it possible for the child to have the best experience in the school.

The early identification of children with special needs because of superior mental ability, specific talents, emotional problems, or even mental retardation calls for a greater emphasis upon techniques of observation and screening. To an even greater degree than in the secondary school, the teacher is a participant in the pupil personnel program of the school. The teacher is in a most favorable position for observation of behavior and shares with the counselor the responsibility for the identification of children with special needs. Although the counselor in the secondary school works closely with the teacher, there is even greater need in the elementary school for the counselor to become a teacher consultant in matters of pupil motivation and adjustment to the classroom situation. Other specialists who make up the pupil personnel team in the elementary school, and with whom the counselor works closely, are the school social worker, the school psychologist, school nurse or physician, reading and speech specialists, and librarian.

It is difficult to set a specific counselor-student ratio because much depends upon the attitude and confidence of other members of the school staff. The White House Conference recommended the ratio of one counselor to every 600 elementary school pupils. A committee of the American School Counselor Association recommended a ratio of one to 450 pupils. It is clear that these ratios are very rough benchmarks. In a given school there may be a relationship between counselor and teacher and principal, on the one hand, and between counselor and other personnel specialists, on the other, that will permit a higher pupil-counselor ratio. Such a ratio is less significant than *the amount of assistance from all sources in the school that is available to each pupil.*

It is apparent that the elementary school, building upon the experience of the past two or three decades in the development of both elementary and secondary pupil personnel programs, should study its distinctive needs and plan for the future. The American Personnel and Guidance Association initiated in 1961 an extensive study of directions to be taken in this area of school work. The Advisory Commission for the project will doubtless propose some experimental studies that will test varying assumptions now made in elementary school counseling.

## The Elementary School Counselor's Job and Skills

The elementary school counselor engages in four primary activities: pupil study; counseling including the use of planned group situations; consultation with teacher, parents, principal, and other specialists; follow-up studies and evaluative research. In small elementary schools the school counselor will also act as school psychologist and perhaps school social worker. In the larger schools or systems where these specialists are available the counselor uses them as referral resources or may engage in therapeutic counseling or in home visiting under the supervision of the school psychologist or school social worker.

In general, when the genesis of the problem is in the school, or in some combination of school, parent, and teacher, the counselor assumes the primary responsibility for the problem. When the problem is in the home and some change in home conditions or parental attitude is needed, the school social worker comes into the picture. When the problem is too complex as far as the child's psychological make-up is concerned, the school psychologist is the resource person. In the Baltimore County system for example, the elementary school counselors do a good bit of intensive interviewing under the supervision of the school psychologist. The psychologist listens to taped interviews or discusses the child's reaction in play therapy and works with the counselor as he in turn works with the child.

The elementary school counselor must have at least three specialized capacities which are unique in type or degree from those expected of the secondary school counselor (a) He must be able to communicate with the child in a nonverbal manner such as observations of play tasks because the younger child may lack the words necessary to express feelings about himself and others. (b) He must be able to work skillfully in the area of reading diagnosis and of emotional problems that may accompany poor reading. The emotional involvement that is frequently associated with poor reading may be either cause or effect, but the relationship between the two requires an essential kind of understanding upon the part of the elementary school counselor. (c) He must be able to work skillfully with parents, both as a counselor and as a small group leader, since the parent-child relationship is of extreme importance to the elementary school child and to his school development.

## Vocational Counseling

The elementary school and the junior high school have more urgent need in the immediate future than in the past for

150

stressing vocational information and vocational counseling for a portion of their student population. Educational requirements to enter an increasing number of occupations will go up too rapidly to permit the rapidly growing youth population to keep up with the requirements unless systematic professional help is provided. A major recommendation of several of the 1960 White House Conference groups was for an increase in work orientation and work-school experience of pupils in the upper elementary and junior high school grades.

In general, the person who has only completed elementary school or a portion of high school will find it increasingly difficult to get permanent vocational placement, yet some of the metropolitan areas will see increasing *numbers* of students dropping out when the compulsory school age limit is reached. In Washington, D. C., the District Council on Human Relations recommended an increase of $600,000 in the 1960 public school budget for expanded vocational counseling and training to better prepare Negro youths for earning a living. The District Commissioners were urged to employ 100 additional counselors on the elementary school level and to begin vocational training at the junior high school level, rather than to wait until the senior high school. The same District Council on Human Relations recommended the additional employment of 32 counselors in the junior high schools.

## Two Illustrations of Programs

The programs that have been developing in the New York City school system entitled "Early Identification and Prevention Program" and "Higher Horizons Program" illustrate the developing nature of the elementary school counselor's work. In the Early Identification Program, the counselor works as a full-time member of a team containing himself, a half-time school social worker, and a half-time school psychologist. The team works exclusively with children in grades kindergarten through third grade in the identification of both positive and negative characteristics, those which both contribute to and detract from the learning process in the early school years. In the Higher Horizons Program the attempt is made not only to identify and stimulate talent in elementary school and junior high school but to provide a program of cultural enrichment through resources found both in the school and in the community.

That the positive approach as opposed to the restrictive and problem-shooting emphasis can appeal to teachers is illustrated in a study made of one of the Bakersfield, California, city schools. The Potomac Elementary School had a heavy enrollment of children from families in the lower socio-economic levels, primarily members of minority groups. After a two-year counseling program of a positive sort the teachers were given questionnaires similar to those that they had responded to at the beginning of the program regarding the various features of the program. At the end of the two years teacher reaction to the plan showed these marked changes: the teacher's desire for the counselor to engage in "stronger discipline and a less psychological approach" decreased from 70 per cent at the beginning of the program to 20 per cent at the end of the second year. The two years experience with the program resulted also in a greater demand for suggestions to help the teacher and for talks by the counselor in the classroom. More than 50 per cent of the teachers requested "additional information concerning the counselor's work and information about children referred from their respective classes."

## The Systematic Development of Pupil Personnel Services

The *student* is the central figure in the school and next to him in importance is the *teacher*. The *school principal* is administratively responsible for everything that happens in a school and for its relations to the community. These points of unassailable fact must be held in mind as pupil personnel services are considered. It must also be remembered that the parent is the person most concerned and most responsible for the individual student. Schools and their staff do not replace the primary importance of the home and parents in the life of the child. The school is a primary agency for society in such matters as intellectual development and vocational planning but it is always secondary to the home in total responsibility for the child or youth.

The counselor's job in the school has always been that of bringing *additional* understandings and skills to the discharge of normal school functions. Provision will be made for the basic elements of a school program whether or not a counselor is present — a curriculum, instruction, evaluation of educational achievement, disposition of individual behavior problems, some kinds of contacts with the community, and the administration of administrative regulations. The counselor or other members of the personnel team, *add to what well-qualified teachers already know* about individual differences, motivational readiness for learning and personality obstacles to learning, necessary adaptations to the education of the handicapped and the gifted, or the effect of classroom activity upon the mental health of the student.

Beyond this, the counselor, because he possesses some unique psychological understandings, brings *specialized competencies* and understandings in such matters as individual psychological dynamics and the interaction of members of a group. The counselor brings competencies in vocational appraisal which contribute to improved student self-understanding and planning. He knows how psychological tests should be used and not used. He brings skills in interviewing and case study techniques. He sees how mental health understandings can be applied to staff as well as pupils; he contributes to the growth of a parent's understanding of the child's characteristics and possible future. A 1958 committee of the American Psychological Association on Relations between Psychology and Education describes 20 of these pupil personnel services under the headings of (1) individual pupil development, (2) general school climate, and (3) relations with community groups and individuals.

The school counselor is the focus of this report. He is, however, only one of several pupil personnel specialists, ordinarily the first one to appear in the school. He, or several counselors, contributes as many as possible of these additions to normal school functions until other personnel specialists are added such as a school psychologist or school social worker. Then the functions are divided and more attention is given to each of them. When the counselor is the only personnel specialist available he is spread thin, even on strictly personnel functions, but this he must do until help arrives. So a counselor *is* the pupil personnel program in some schools.

The development of an embryo pupil personnel program to a more mature one embodies several moves, sometimes taken serially, sometimes simultaneously.

## 1.  *Improvement of Quality of Counseling*

This is an early step. It may mean movement of a qualified counselor from a part-time to a full-time status. Currently this is a common step. The focus should be, however, upon the *quality* of the counseling provided, not upon a mere increase in numbers of counselors. One criterion at a minimum level is that all counselors in the school meet the state counselor certification requirements in the 38 states where certification is in effect. Such requirements are frequently minimal in a real sense of the word particularly if there are no levels of competency provided for in the certification regulations.

Although amount and kind of professional preparation is no guarantee of improved effectiveness, the probability is increased if counselors are prepared beyond minimal levels and in the areas outlined in the next chapter. Such preparation is essential if the counselor is to keep abreast of changing social and educational conditions.

Another way in which quality may be improved is the development of a *policy* which clarifies the functions of the counselor and other pupil personnel workers and their relationship to teachers and administrators. The policy could well be developed on the initiative of the staff and most certainly with their understanding, as well as with the approval of the superintendent of schools and the school board. In the view of this report, such a policy should provide that a major part of the counselor's time with students be reserved for constructive work for students who are not at a crisis point, for work having a developmental rather than a remedial emphasis. It means also an expectation that much of his remaining time shall be given to teachers, principal, and parents in assisting them to fulfill their goals for students and to understand better the students with whom they deal.

The development of a counseling policy, understood by both the counselor and by those who work with him, is essential unless much counselor time is to be wasted in attempts to meet impossible and unwise expectations. Policy regarding the counselor's job could well be a part of a policy understanding regarding the work of all pupil personnel workers. The point at which most confusion arises, however, is the specific work of the counselor. This is because teachers have counseling responsibilities as well and because the counselor must work closely with teachers in the development of all students.

### 2. *Continuing Analysis of Student Body and Community*

This significant move can either precede or follow that described under 1. Such a demographic study of changing student population characteristics should be accompanied by ecological studies of changes in the community that influence student culture and student needs. Likewise essential is the study of the movement of students from a particular school to the next educational unit or their movement to entry vocations. Once there is acceptance of *the need for study* of the facts about students now in school, about those who will be enrolling within the next year or two, about those who have left, about the community out of which they come, the specifics of the research involved will adjust themselves for a given school situation.

The counselor may not be the person who collects the actual data — a research agency in the system or a committee of counselors and teachers may carry out the study. But the counselor more than any other should interpret the data in terms of student needs and possible program implications. Most important, perhaps, is the impact of such information upon curriculum. Translation of needs into curriculum changes is the job of a curriculum council or committee upon which the counselor may serve as a consultant. Beyond this, however, the implications of student population and community research data seem clear for such school action as: the orientation of new students; the provision of environmental information essential to education and career planning; the provision of adequate personnel records; the adequacy of health services; the effectiveness of whatever job placement service exists, the use of the community's agencies for school needs, etc.

## 3. *Provision for Coordination of Services*

For some schools and systems, this step could come earlier in the development, particularly if some of the other steps have already been undertaken, or if various personnel and services require coordination. Two types of leadership are called for. In the first, the coordination of professional personnel is effected by a professional pupil personnel worker — counselor, school psychologist, school social worker, etc. A director of pupil personnel services should be a person professionally trained in some one of the pupil personnel services. Since the work of the counselor deliberately covers the total school program and the total school population, more frequently than not he will be given responsibility for this coordination. The primary consideration is that this is professional leadership by a professional person.

The second type is administrative leadership. This may be given by a general administrator who depends upon the professional staff involved for matters of policy and professional direction. In a given school the vice principal would not only provide administrative leadership for the professional staff but would also be responsible for relating pupil personnel work to the total school program and for integrating the special services to the best advantage of the instructional and administrative program. He would be concerned with seeing that the pupil personnel specialists relate their efforts to those of the teaching and administrative staff who are carrying out related functions associated with student adjustment and development both in and out of the classroom. Preferably such a vice principal or assistant superintendent might have had his own preparation and experience in the field of one of the pupil personnel services. This is not essential if he has respect for the nature of the professional training possessed by those who will work within the program. Such an assistant superintendent or vice principal would depend upon the director of pupil personnel, senior counselor, or senior personnel worker, much as the vice president of a university depends upon the dean of the college for academic leadership or the dean of students for understanding of the student body.

Such a division of the coordination responsibilities may not be necessary if (1) the vice principal or associate superintendent

155

is qualified in pupil personnel work and has this as his major responsibility and if (2) the administrative responsibilities of this position do not crowd out the provision of leadership in stimulating the professional imagination and the personal growth of the staff. Effective counselors are too frequently lured into administrative posts where they may become less effective administrators. One severe drain upon the present supply of school counselors is just of this order.

The counselor's need for recognition and status — as common to counselors as to other people — may be met by the possibility of his becoming a professional leader without being required to assume the role of a general school administrator. Status and self-satisfaction may also be gained by the completion of research studies or the recognition by others that he is a skillful counselor. Counselors need some tangible signs of acceptance and recognition, but the present movement toward administrative status as the only possibilty is not healthy for their profession. Nor can a mature and effective counselor be replaced easily. The distinction between *professional leadership* and *administrative responsibility* is proposed as good for the school and good for most counselors.

4. *School Resources for a Counseling Program*

A determination of the adequacy of total pupil personnel resources within the school parallels the study of student characteristics. A simple addition of counselors is not the answer nor is the attainment of some specified counselor-student ratio. The number of counselors needed depends upon the other resources within the school, resources as inclusive as the teacher's feelings of responsibility for student welfare, appropriately varied curricular offerings, and school organization policies that are meaningful from the students' point of view.

*Counselor-Student Ratio.* A suggested ratio of one full-time counselor to each 300 pupils would be adequate in some schools and would be inadequate in others. Even under good circumstances, however, a high school should not indicate that it has an adequate counseling program if it does not have at least one qualified counselor in this ratio. No school, for example, would indicate that it had a health service unless a qualified medical staff was available for a substantial portion of the time. A one-period-a-day counselor does not justify a statement that the school has a counseling program any more than a nurse for one period a day or a doctor present two hours a week would justify an assumption of a health service.

Perhaps more to the point as a criterion is the proportion of time made available for the counselor to engage in two of his primary functions. In the secondary school it is recom-

156

mended that each school counselor have at least 50 per cent of his time available for working with individual students, or with groups of students in what has been defined as "planned group experiences," and 25 per cent of his time for working with teaching staff and administration. This ratio would shift for the elementary school counselor where it is recommended that at least one-third of his time be allocated to working with students and at least one-half of his time to work with staff and other resource personnel.

In the time spent with staff and with principal the counselor should be encouraged to do more than meet day-to-day problems but to serve also as an innovator and a producer of new ideas out of his knowledge of students and student life. It is inefficient to have the counselor's time spent in dealing only with individual teacher-student problems or questions that the principal has about a given student. He should be expected to provide leadership in ideas that grow out of his knowledge of student life and human relations in general, and knowledge of vocational and social conditions.

*Educational and Vocational Information.* The presence and accessibility of current information on educational opportunities and the changing vocational requirements is an essential factor in the counselor's program. This means provisions for keeping such information current and up to date and provision for its interpretation to both students and staff. This may be done by the counselor's use of the group process, through regular classes as parts of the curriculum, and through automated provisions for the materials to be kept current and in condition for use by students and counselors.

Educational differentiation will increase in significance within the near future in response to societal demands for individuals with technological skills of a substantial order as well as demands for scientists and for professional people in human relations occupations. There will certainly be a longer period of basic formal education and the kinds of education available will be more varied.

There is need that the information on further educational opportunities be specific regarding the social and academic climate of the future school unit and the personal satisfactions that may be expected there. This is in addition to the normal information about admissions requirements and costs. Some of this information may be known only by the counselor, but every attempt should be made to provide such information in a form that encourages its use directly by students and teachers.

A similar situation exists with regard to vocational information. Here again the school will be judged in terms of the adequacy of its plan for providing a flow of current information on changing conditions in the occupational world. It may be anticipated that occupational change data will increasingly be collated by both federal and state agencies. The school's plan to utilize such service will be a criterion for an adequate pupil personnel program.

There will be pressures upon the school and upon the counselor to assume responsibility for manpower distribution in the interests of the nation. The counselor should know well the manpower needs of the nation and these should be transmitted to the student but without pressure upon him "to go where he is needed." The counselor is responsible for seeing that the student is *informed* about vocational change and national need but not for seeing that national manpower quotas are filled. To make the position of this report quite clear, it is stated that the counselor must not direct the student vocationally or otherwise if he is to maintain his role as counselor.

A study of the more effective school use of information about occupations was undertaken for the U. S. Office of Education by L. O. Brockmann. His report points out that career materials are an integral part of total curriculum resources and that audio-visual aids, especially educational TV and radio, ought to be used more dramatically. These are ideal for the purpose of helping young people actually see the nature of occupations which they are considering. He points out that work-experience educational programs are undertaken in far too small a number of high schools, possibly 2,000 throughout the country.

The usual discussion of job clusters is given new emphasis by Brockmann. In particular he suggests that people now shift frequently from one field to the other and that their awareness of the relatedness of jobs would reduce the loss attendant upon such a shift. (This relatedness of vocations is true even in professional groups as Dael Wolfle pointed out in *America's Resources of Specialized Talent.*)

A section of Brockmann's report emphasizes these points in the use of vocational information: (1) Such information should consider the contribution which women make to American social life and to the labor force. So much of the present information is in terms of distinctive jobs for women rather than the consideration of occupations for women that are held by men and women alike. In the latter instance the woman is important as an intelligent member of the labor force, not merely as a woman. (2) The choice must be made by the student even though he has assistance from teachers, counselors, and parents. Parental understanding of their children is essential since parents have so large an influence upon children's vocational choices. (3) The appreciation of things beautiful in music, art, literature, and nature has implications for satisfactions to be gained from certain occupations. (4) Our concept of ethics, fair play, and justice in human relations is an emphasis in our culture which should be given attention in career planning. Career materials need to stress a social responsibility which all persons recognize in their service to our evolving culture. (5) Career materials should be related to dynamic world happenings.

*Additional Program Provisions.* The school should provide also: (a) opportunities for learning from experience in student organizations and learning from planned group experiences where the interaction within the group under leadership is of prime significance; (b) the appropriate orientation of new students; (c) provision for the collection, organization, and interpretation of a body of information about each student that will enable both teacher and counselor to understand and work with students more effectively; (d) provision for health services and vocational placement services to the extent that these are not present in a community or cannot be utilized.

These general program provisions are to be provided under the assumption that the principal, teachers, and counselors all accept responsibility for acting in response to individual differences, have respect for student uniqueness and self-responsibility, and have concern for the best development of individual talent. A quotation from Professors Hugh M. Bell and Clarence A. Mahler, who in 1959 made an evaluation of the pupil personnel services in the Portland, Oregon, schools, provides an appropriate flavor for the conclusion of this chapter:

> It is apparent that in a democracy the choice of a school course of study and the career to which it leads must be permissive, must provide pupils and their parents freedom to accept or reject a particular curriculum or career. . . . The necessity for guidance arises out of the immaturity of developing youth, on the one hand, and the complexity of modern society on the other. Educating youth in the art and science of making wise decisions at the various stages of development becomes the central task of an effective guidance service.

# The School Counselor—Professional and Personal

## CONTENTS

# It Is Recommended:

1. That state certifying agencies for counselors and graduate faculties in counselor education specify that, in addition to essential professional courses and experiences, two other major cores be required in the counselor education curriculum; one major core is in the field of psychology, another in the social and other behavioral sciences, the two combined to represent a minimum of from one-third to one-half of the course work required for certification.

2. That the minimal two-year graduate program in counselor education include: (a) two major cores in psychology and the social sciences as described in Recommendation 1; (b) adequate orientation in educational philosophy and school curriculum patterns; (c) applied or professional courses as described in the text to the extent of *not more* than one-fourth of the total graduate programs; (d) supervised experience in both counseling and planned group leadership to the extent of *not less* than one-fourth of the total graduate programs; (e) an introduction to the understanding and utilization of changing research concepts; (f) an introduction to the problems of ethical relationships and legal responsibilities in counseling.

3. That the graduate courses in counselor education be taught by faculty qualified in the respective areas involved, *i.e.*, psychology courses by psychologists; counseling theory and technique courses by faculty who are both qualified in psychology and experienced in counseling; social science courses by social scientists; occupational information, psychological measurement, and research courses by qualified scholars in the areas involved.

4. That supervised counseling experience be required in every pattern of counselor certification; that certification be granted only upon the satisfactory completion of this experience and the recommendation of the graduate faculty involved.

5. That state certifying agencies for counselors and graduate faculties in counselor education understand that, although most counselors will continue to have a background in teaching, there is a rich reservoir of talent for counseling in fields other than teaching. Teaching experience is not always essential, provided there is required a substantial block of supervised counseling experience in a school setting.[1]

6. That the counselor certification requirements in each state be viewed as minimal and be periodically re-examined in the light of changing educational and social conditions and changing standards of quality performance in counseling. This examination and the statement of appropriate modifications should involve the coordinated effort of the state department of education, state professional associations, and the graduate counselor education faculties of the state.

7. That counselors be prepared whose specific function will be to assist adults in educational and vocational planning and personal adjustment as they resume formal education at different periods in their lifetime.

8. That school counselors consider that their professional education, both broadly and specifically conceived, is never complete; that they give such continuing attention to a broadening of their cultural development that the amount of time devoted to reading, travel, concerts, and similar activities be even more than that given to professional up-dating.

[1] Dugald Arbuckle registers a dissent to the use of the last four words of this recommendation. He would omit these words. Kenneth A. Erickson registers a dissent to the last sentence of this recommendation.

## CHAPTER 7

# *The School Counselor—Professional and Personal*

THE PRECEDING chapters have proposed not only that the counselor is the focal point in the guidance program, but that counseling is his major job. A great many other activities now expected of him seriously detract from his ability to help students and to serve as a skillful consultant to the staff on matters of student development. The concept of "a guidance program" as a distinct adjunct to instructional and administrative functions has been narrowing in focus with increasing attention to the counselor's responsibility for counseling. Many features of the program have been absorbed within the total school program and more will be absorbed as the philosophy of guidance is accepted as the philosophy of the school. The term "guidance worker," already in disfavor, will disappear from our vocabulary as a vague and ambiguous term involving a person whose time must be spread so thinly over such a variety of activities that no one of them can be performed adequately. The specialized preparation of such a worker is impossibly comprehensive.

Such were the conclusions drawn in the preceding chapters. The counselor must prepare to counsel students in a rapidly changing culture. As demanding as this task is, the counselor will do more than work with students. He will work with and assist others who influence the school life and the development of the student — teachers, parents, administrators. He will study current student characteristics and the changes taking place in school populations, and interpret these to curriculum and administration committees. He will work with and perhaps coordinate the work of other pupil personnel specialists, will effect liaison with community resources for student adjustment and development. He must be scholarly as well as effective in interpersonnel relations, work with both head and heart.

Clearly the counselor must be professionally educated and not merely "trained." Like the minister or physician or any other educated professional, he must learn specialized procedures and be responsible for their application in the light of a broad knowledge of his field. The school counselor, of course, will continue to exist at several levels of development and competency. Not all will become masters. Journeymen and apprentices will continue to outnumber the fully qualified counselors that are described later in this chapter in terms of their qualifications and education. But unless the highest standards are established for the profession, there can be no clearly defined program for either the qualified master counselor or the journeyman.

## What Counselors Recommend

Before considering some basic recommendations it may be well to examine what is said by the counselors and counselor educators in the three studies introduced in Chapter 5.

### Educational Background of School Counselors

The professional education of counselors has been advanced materially during the past decade. For many counselors, however, the advance has not been personal experience. When the backgrounds of the 1,200 counselors studied for this report are examined, preparation in some vital areas is sparse in spite of the large proportion having a master's degree. Most counselors have a substantial background in psychology but from 11 per cent to 36 per cent of the three groups of counselors have had none. Still more have had no graduate work in the social sciences and in supervised practicum experience. In particular, the counselors found in the Project TALENT random sampling of high schools across the country have a limited educational background. Twenty-one per cent have had not even one graduate course in counseling, 28 per cent no course in psychological measurement, and 43 per cent none in occupational information. In the roughly comparable areas of the three studies of counselors are these percentages:

|  | TALENT Counselors | ASCA Counselors | Elementary Counselors |
|---|---|---|---|
| Per Cent with No Graduate Practicum | 70 | 48 | 43 |
| No Sociology or Economics Course | 79 | 39 | 31 |
| No Psychology Course | 36 | 11 | 17 |

When the high school counselors of the ASCA study and the elementary school counselors were asked about the future, both groups recommended more preparation in psychology and more supervised experience on the practicum level. (Detailed figures are found in Table 4 on page 195).

### Counselor-Educators Look at the Future

In the projections by the 32 counselor-educators who cooperated with the Commission no one's phrasing and emphasis duplicated any other's but some emphases were held in common by a sizable proportion of the group. A preface to the listing of statements should make clear that almost all agreed upon *a minimum of two years of graduate work* and *a considerable broadening* of both graduate and undergraduate curriculums. More specifically they recommended increased attention to:

|  | | Number of Counselor-Educators (N = 32) |
|---|---|---|
| 1. | Psychological understandings (developmental, child psychology, personality dynamics, etc.) | 21 |
| | Adult and group psychology (of parents, teachers, etc.) | 11 |
| | Psychological appraisal (measurement, developmental patterns, etc.) | 11 |
| | Counseling theory and procedures | 7 |
| 2. | Societal conditions (cultural changes, sociology, anthropology, etc.) | 19 |
| | A markedly broader education | 10 |
| 3. | Practicum (supervised experience, internship, etc.) | 15 |
| 4. | Research competencies | 10 |
| 5. | Values and ethical understandings | 4 |
| 6. | Counselor self-understanding | 4 |

It is clear that increased psychological understandings, a broader education in social and cultural conditions, supervised experience in counseling, and competency in research stand out in these projections. Such groupings of responses do an injustice to the cogency and imagination evident in some of the responses. These three quotations illustrate the imagination shown in many of the responses.

1. In 1980 the school counselor will be much more intimately a part of the total educational effort than he is now. He will be concerned with school as a social organism planned to help all children achieve maximum self-realization. He will not be primarily concerned with abilities, interests, and jobs, but more centrally with projecting life patterns in a society. He will be more of a psychologist and more of a social critic. He will see his role as an aid to individuals in synthesizing experience as a basis for planning new experience.

2. Counselor competencies will include thorough knowledge of the psychology of personality development, sources of difficulty and their remediation, knowledge of philosophical and value dimensions, skill in counseling (not only with personal difficulties but also with clarification and development of aspirations and maturity), knowledge of testing. Stressed will be supervised experience in counseling so that counselors will become aware of their own tendencies as well as client characteristics, and will develop sensitive counseling skills.

Another way to get at a changed trend is to say that up to now counseling has been pretty much oriented toward getting a student up to grade, to be normal, to learn to conform or to succeed (in conforming). A new emphasis in counseling will be to help individuals to develop individuality, personally discovered value systems, skills in making personal judgments in a somewhat chaotic world.

3.  By 1980 we will have learned first to identify the bipolarity of our thinking and then discover ways of avoiding that bipolarity. I refer to the desirable objective measurement movement, which substituted for the un-enlightened sentimentality of the Horatio Alger legend in the early days of guidance. But in some respects we have become such a highly technical and professionally self-conscious group of workers, that we may have lost some of the personal touch that is so necessary in our Western brand of education.

What we now know in a more sophisticated manner about the use of warm relationships to cultivate motivation needs to be emphasized in order to avoid impersonal, commercial-like relationships with our clientele. Medicine faces a similar problem of being required, on the one hand, to be increasingly scientific and hard-headed in searching for causes, and at the same time being perceived by the patient as highly personal and really friendly. As more research is done in our field and as we increasingly stuff graduate students full of research findings, we will need to take steps to ensure that counselors know that they are dealing with living human beings.

This means analyzing the content of our training programs to see whether or not we are pumping in any content that re-emphasizes the humanness of our clientele. Perhaps we ought to borrow from the humanities, philosophy and anthropology, as well as from psychology, in order to get at the humanness of the relationship in the midst of the scientific analysis of that relationship. This need not be as paradoxical as it sounds.

## The Professional Education of the Future Counselor

Graduate counselor education currently focuses upon psychological understanding and will, of course, continue to do so. There will be an expansion beyond the individual differences, and test and measurement level which describes too large a proportion of current curricula. It is now seen that psychological preparation must include knowledge and skill in understanding and dealing with individual behavior dynamics and with the psychological dynamics operating in small groups. There must be an educated sensitivity to the nuances of human behavior, as well as a solid grounding in developmental psychology and the environmental influences bearing upon that development. This much and more is made clear in Chapter 3.

The second major development in graduate education for counselors involves study of the immediate culture of the community, the larger culture of the nation, and the various cultures of the world. This must have a reference point in time as well as in space so that the past illumines the present. Such understanding will require study in sociology, economics, anthropology, international relations, and other areas — perhaps with somewhat less emphasis than is given to the study of individual and small group human behavior. This social understanding, however, must extend considerably beyond the present emphasis upon a knowledge of existing vocational structure and college admission requirements as is made clear in Chapter 2.

A third emphasis grows out of the proposal that counselors work almost as much with other school people and with parents as they do with students. This means up-to-date understanding of school purpose, organization, curriculum, and instructional procedures. The counselor must know what is taking place in education much as is suggested in Chapter 4. Beyond this the counselor must have some grounding in adult psychology and parental education.

A fourth major task for the counselor growing out of this report calls for at least minimal understanding of research procedures and cautions. The counselor must keep a constant investigative eye upon the student population and the changes in community influences that bear upon the characteristics of that population. If someone else does the studies he must be able to interpret with appropriate caution and meaning. The counselor does not become a research worker necessarily but he must know how to seek, analyze, and interpret research information. This is brought out in Chapters 5 and 6.

The above considerations must be related to what is considered valid in present-day counselor education. In particular, attention must be given to the relative time allotments of different aspects of the graduate program. Pulling together all that has been said it is proposed that a *minimal two-year graduate program include the following:*

1. One major core in psychology, including developmental and child psychology, personality growth and dynamics, and group psychology.
2. A second major core in the study of societal forces and culture changes involving the graduate areas of sociology, anthropology, economics, and international relations. This core could be based upon undergraduate preparation in any of the natural sciences, social sciences, or humanities. The relation of the undergraduate program to the graduate years in the liberating and scientific disciplines is given further attention in the later section on "Teaching Experience." Depending upon the strength of the undergraduate program in the social sciences and psychology,

167

*from one-third to one-half* of the total graduate program should be devoted to these two major core areas.

3. An understanding of the basic educational philosophies and school curriculum patterns.

4. Provision for the essential applied or technique courses in counseling, measurement, educational and occupational information, etc., to the extent of *not more* than one-fourth of the total graduate program. The preparation for psychological appraisal would stress research knowledge of the tests used and attention to life history analysis. In the area of occupational information emphasis would be placed on the psychological factors entering into vocational choice and the differential meaning of occupational information to each student. There can, of course, be no substitute for *a rigorous study of the world of occupations* as they exist today and as they are projected into the immediate future. Educational information would examine ways in which counselors would determine the distinctive intellectual and social climate of the school to which the student might transfer.

5. Supervised experience in both individual counseling and planned group situations to the extent of *not less* than one-fourth of the total graduate program. The supervision would be by a combination of graduate school staff and well-qualified counselors in the school who were carefully selected and appointed as part of the graduate school team. The goal would be paid internships on an academic-year basis.

6. An elementary understanding of research methods and cautions, including an introduction to electronic computer programming and the outcomes to be expected from computer use.

7. Introduction to the problems of ethical relationships and legal responsibilities in counseling.

## The Counselor as a Person

Although not part of any official curriculum, the graduate faculty in counselor education should give attention to the need for personal psychological growth of graduate students in this field. The counselor as a person is the most important single factor in counseling. He needs to understand himself psychologically in order to be effective in helping others. He does not need to be, perhaps should not be, balanced in all ways so that he lacks distinctiveness. He needs to know how to *control* his biases and defenses so that they do not interfere with the progress of any person with whom he is working.

The counselor needs to be socially sensitive and flexible, imaginative, with good control of both his intellectual activity and his emotions. Yet achieving this is a lifetime process as it is discussed in the last section of this report. In any event, assistance to him in this connection is a legitimate and essention concern of the graduate years. Such help cannot be legislated or required — it must be sought by the individual. And it may take on any one of several forms — help by a faculty member, by a professional counselor in the counseling center, or by a psychiatrist in the university student health service, help through an informal group devoted to a consideration of professional and personal growth problems, help through group counseling or group psychotherapy that is directed by a professionally equipped person. Provision of such facilities, for use on an encouraged but voluntary basis, is as important as any other laboratory facility that is provided such as a one-way vision room for interviewing. In fact, help of the sort suggested here is *particularly* appropriate as the graduate student faces up to himself in supervised interview experience.

## The Undergraduate Program and Teaching Experience

The major theme of this report is that counselors must be broadly educated and be understanding of the constantly shifting cultural pattern. In any consideration of the program outlined in this chapter it becomes readily apparent that too much is being expected of even a two-year program of graduate study. Some of the basic understandings must be secured in the undergraduate program, while others become refinements to be sought in graduate school and as a part of a program of continuing education throughout the counselor's professional lifetime. It seems apparent that the broad cultural basing of the counselor must be seen in reference to the undergraduate experience. The counselor for the schools of tomorrow needs a cultural education of some breadth coupled with intensive study in some area. The person who has majored in the sciences, in the humanities, or in the social sciences, and has become deeply aware of the cultural and scientific changes taking place in at least one of these broad areas will be in a position to build an adequate graduate program in preparation for counseling.

### The Teaching Certificate and Teaching Experience

The relationship between the undergraduate program, the teaching certificate, and teaching experience is an obvious one. The counselor needs to gain as much knowledge as possible of the world of man and nature through his undergraduate program if he is to build well his graduate program. He also needs certain kinds of pertinent experience to work effectively as a counselor in a school setting. It has been taken for granted that the counselor can secure this experience only as a paid teacher. This requires a teaching certificate, which in turn requires that some of the undergraduate time be taken for this purpose. Does this unduly rob the undergraduate program of time that is needed for cultural broadening? If experience is needed for counseling, then is paid teaching experience the *only* kind that can be utilized?

It is true, of course, that the professional courses required for a teacher's certificate make up a relatively minor part of the total pattern of undergraduate work. The typical requirement of around 20 semester hours out of a total of 120 undergraduate hours does not seem an undue amount of emphasis for securing a high school teacher's thorough-going orientation to the school process and school structure. A considerable share of these hours are spent in educational psychology and educational philosophy with less time devoted to what could be called techniques courses than is commonly understood. Nor are the so-called "methods" courses divorced of subject matter of teaching content, since the professional course is often a working combination of the two. Without questioning too seriously the legitimacy of teaching certificate requirements for teachers they are questioned for counselors if "teaching experience" is the justification. The question might be asked in this manner: "Should lack of a teaching certificate and paid teaching experience bar from school counseling those who may be otherwise qualified to counsel students and consult with staff?"

This issue can be resolved only after considering a more basic question: "What kind of a person should this counselor be, if he is to be trusted and relied upon by staff as well as students?" Professor Robert Mathewson, director of counselor education in the New York City Municipal Colleges, believes that the job demands, and the school principal wants, basic qualities of *maturity* and of *personal understanding*. These may derive from a range of life experiences, including preferably some kind of experience in schools. This is probably a more satisfactory statement than the listing of any of the traits found in numberless statements of opinion on the subject. Not only is the validity of the opinions regarding desirable traits wholly unknown, but the trait approach is a sadly outdated one.

The 32 graduate counselor-educators who cooperated in the Commission's study were asked the question noted in Chapter 5, "What will be the emphasis upon counselor competencies and preparation 20 years from now?" *Not one* of the educators mentioned teaching experience or any particular kind of experience as a preparation requirement. Perhaps they all took "teaching experience" for granted as a requirement for the future, but the writer's personal knowledge of some of the respondents would not support this conclusion. The qualities demanded include such factors as "Broader education and experience — longer period of preparation"; "A basic understanding of the curricular experiences available"; "Sensitivity to society and its dynamics"; "Better understanding of early childhood"; "Much more knowledgeable about society than counselors of today"; "Sensitivity to everything that is going on in the intangible area of human relationships and to the complex *meanings* of what is said by word and gesture."

If these suggested competencies are subsumed under the categories of "maturity" and "experience" it is to be noted that no limitation was placed by any educator on the manner in which they are developed. This returns us to the earlier question: If the professional task of the school counselor calls for personal qualities presumably contributed to by experience, must this be only paid teaching experience that calls for the usual teacher preparation? Two thoughtful statements bear upon this question. Dean John Fischer (for many years the Superintendent of Schools in Baltimore) writes, "Actual classroom experience is less important for a counselor than his knowledge of the role of the school in our society, the functions of different kinds of schools, the nature of learning, and the specific purposes of various elements in the curriculum. If in a prospective counselor I could have all of these things (professional education and personal qualities) in addition to successful teaching experience I should be very pleased. But I would not allow the requirement of prior teaching experience to limit my field of choice to a point where I would have to take second- or third-rate people." Yet there is very real danger that the specific requirement of paid teaching experience might provide a serious limitation in the choices available.

The 1958 report of the Committee on Professional Training, Licensing, and Certification of APGA points out that state certification regulations stress only *amount* of experience and not its quality or nature. In criticizing this limitation the report states: "Future research may indicate that some kinds of work experience are actually detrimental. Many able persons may decide not to enter counseling as a career because of experience requirements which are too demanding and which, in fact, may have little validity. The Committee suggests that other kinds of experience, such as leisure time and volunteer activities, might provide the same skills and understanding which supposedly result from employment."

171

Three patterns for securing desirable experience are proposed:

a. Teaching certificate and teaching experience of one to four years (a longer experience in dealing with group situations and using instructional procedures may be disadvantageous in shifting from teacher role to counselor role). Graduate study and supervised counseling experience may be added during or following this experience.

b. Directly following the undergraduate degree, to enroll for two years of graduate study one of which will be full time internship or supervised experience in a school setting similar to that in which the student-counselor wishes to work. This would include observing and assisting teachers in classroom duties. Following this the student could be employed as a "junior counselor" for one or two further years before assumption of full fledged counselor responbility.

c. Undergraduate education followed by (1) several years experience in any one of many life experiences (occupations, volunteer activity, travel, etc.) which contribute directly to knowledge of human behavior and society and (2) graduate study and one year of full-time supervised experience that acquaints him with the total school program and with teaching and counseling as parts of that program.

Experience which contributes to a desirable maturity of outlook and skill in interpersonal relations is essential. What is questioned here is whether a paid teaching job is the *only* way to gain such experience. Knowledge of the school and the classroom is equally essential but this report proposes that there may be other ways of gaining it than by serving as a full-time classroom teacher. Teaching experience as such, in fact, may result in the teacher's knowing little about the school program beyond the walls of his classroom and the department involved.

We may conclude that paid teaching experience is only one desirable prerequisite to education and employment as a counselor. If other types of experience are also acceptable it may be possible for some prospective counselors to enjoy a broader undergraduate base. There is no assurance, of course, that a liberal arts degree results in a "liberal education." Courses do not guarantee intellectual perspective. It is proposed, however, that broad cultural experience, both through classroom and campus experience, both in college and after college, is a necessary and essential base for the educated counselor of the future.

## The Graduate School

It seems clear that graduate schools not only have full responsibility for the pre-service graduate education of counselors but that the graduate faculties involved have responsibility for the establishment of selection standards. If counselors are to be educated and not trained, the graduate school must take the initiative in specifying the desired emphasis at the undergraduate level and in using imagination in the development of the graduate curriculum in this field. The graduate faculty concerned will of course be responsive to action taken by professional associations and to the implications of a continuing flow of research. They should *not* operate independently of school administrators and counselor supervisors in preparing graduate students to meet specific conditions in the occupational field.

A 1959 study published by the U. S. Office of Education indicated that 223 institutions of higher education have a counselor preparation program at the graduate level. The majority of these programs are in institutions classified as "liberal arts and general with one or more professional schools." What is meant here is not certain but it is clear in another part of the classification that only a handful of the institutions involved are teachers colleges or institutions devoted entirely to teacher preparation. On the other hand, almost all of the programs are conducted by departments of education.

The quality of graduate programs in this field depends upon (1) the richness of the total institutional resources and the extent to which they are appreciated and used, (2) the extent to which the graduate faculty involved are professionally qualified for their teaching, advising, and supervisory responsibilities in the program, and (3) a student-faculty ratio for the core faculty in counselor education which permits attention to individual graduate student development and the most effective use of institutional resources in this development.

In October, 1961, the American Personnel and Guidance Association issued a tentative policy statement, "Standards for the Preparation of School Counselors." The statement, based in considerable part upon the point of view represented in this report, presented tentative standards for the content of the graduate curriculum, selection of counselor candidates, supervised experiences in counseling, and institutional resources for counselor education. Two of the proposals in particular call for major shifts in the thinking of the graduate schools offering programs in this field.

### Supervised Experience

One of the common criticisms of the graduate school, discussed by Bernard Berelson in *Graduate Education in the United States*, is that the graduate school does not adequately teach its college-teaching candidates how to teach. The same thing might be said of the counselor education programs which do not adequately prepare the counseling candidates to counsel. It is at this point that the great need for the internship experience or some form of supervised practice enters the picture. About two-thirds of the graduate institutions reported by the U. S. Office of Education have the requirement of practicum internships or supervised practice as part of their masters or doctors programs. Many institutions, however, do not have adequate provisions for supervised practice regardless of their inclusion of it in their catalogue statements.

The great problem has been the shortage of prepared supervisors in the schools or other agencies where practice is to be secured. Furthermore, supervision of this kind is costly. Large blocks of time are required of the graduate staff member if he is to procure and to keep in touch with the graduate supervisors in schools or other agencies, and if he is to secure the necessary feedback from the graduate student to the department. If the graduate student is to get full benefit from his experience, he should have at a minimum a weekly conference with his graduate supervisor at the university and a weekly seminar with his adviser and his intern colleagues. Jointly listening to tape recordings of interviews or going over in detail recent experiences with a student-client is equivalent to teaching a class of one. This is expensive but without this internship the graduate program will never become effective in its preparation of school counselors. It is one of the most essential developments of the near future, second only to the inclusion in the graduate program of substantial attention to the social sciences and to the broadly cultural development of the counselor.

## A Broadening of Professional Education

Attention to the broad education of the counselor demands a graduate school program that extends beyond the work of the sponsoring department. In August, 1960, the U. S. Office of Education sponsored a conference in counselor education. Among other statements in their report is this one: "There is an increasing recognition of the fact that counselor skill and competencies should be based on a foundation of basic theory and research in the social and behavioral sciences. . . . The assumption that counselor education can be isolated in one department or curriculum is unrealistic. It calls rather for interdisciplinary approach in which the contributions of the behavioral and social sciences are brought to bear on the education of counselors."

Provision of a breadth of education and adequate supervised experience require a basic modification of counselor-education programs in even the major graduate schools of the country.

## Certification Requirements

Counselor certificate requirements in the 38 states having such requirements in 1960 are of value in indicating minimum levels of expectation. There is a considerable public concern for insuring the employment of qualified counselors (in 34 of the states the certification is mandatory not optional; in 15 of the 16 states where there is certification for school psychologists the certification is mandatory) but the qualifications are minimal. They give few cues for future development, few indications of frontier thinking. Certification necessarily follows professional standards, does not lead. Certification provides a floor of minimum standards, but seldom reflects the newer developments of even the graduate institutions in that state. In the process of securing passage of legislation many compromises are made with the forward-looking provisions that may characterize the first draft. What results is a pattern of minimum essentials that are currently acceptable to the variety of people involved in the legislative or board enactment.

An analysis of certification patterns is therefore not particularly useful in projecting professional education patterns into the future. A picture of the requirements suggests a sizable gap between present legal requirements and the expectations of future counselor competencies.

A little over one-half (20) of the 38 certification patterns require a master's degree. The number of graduate hours vary from none to 30. Only 16 of the states have a clearly specified number of graduate hours with the majority having professional course requirements extending over both undergraduate and graduate levels.

The pattern of required courses in the 38 certification programs also leaves something to be desired when the course titles are examined. Of the seven courses that are required in *one-half or more of the programs* (from a study made by C. E. Burckel) four could be labeled as technique courses — "counseling techniques," "individual analysis," "principles and practices of guidance," "organization and administration of guidance." Two of the remaining three could be classified as substantive in nature — "psychology" under many titles, and "mental hygiene." The seventh course could be either — "occupational and educational information." To be remembered is that course titles provide only a suggestion of the emphasis of the course and this classification may lack validity. There is an unhappy possibility, however, that this classification is accurate or even unduly optimistic.

When courses of a substantial nature are further examined we find 14 states specifying "sociology" and 16 "research methods or statistics," but only 7 requiring "economics," 5 "family life," 3 "personality development," and 1 "culture patterns." The techniques emphasis remains overwhelming.

All certification plans except 6 require teaching experience, while 13 specify counseling experience or some combination of teaching, counseling, or social work experience. The requirement of nonteaching work experience in 24 of the certification patterns is an anachronism, at least an unproved assumption. It may actually be harmful as suggested by a Committee of the American Personnel and Guidance Association (see page 171). Vocational counselors should depend upon *their work experience* far less than formerly because it is so much more rapidly outdated. What was experienced in 1950 may be misleading for 1970.

The current state certification requirements are generally limited, unimaginative, and tied to the past. The rapid increase since World War II in the number of states requiring some standards for counselors should not be depreciated. This has been a healthy movement. The "look forward" theme of this report does not, however, secure much assistance from certification plans. They are, and will be in the future, substantial statements of well-accepted and therefore minimal standards. The "new" must seek its source elsewhere.

## Teamwork in Setting Standards of Counselor Performance and Education

It is obvious that many people and agencies are concerned with standards for counselor performance and counselor education. Already named are graduate counselor-educators and certifying agencies such as state departments of education. Deeply involved as well are school administrators and professional organizations in student personnel.

*The School Administrator and the Counselor-Educator*

The school administrator plays a unique and important role in determining standards of counselor performance and education. It is he who accepts the counselor functions proposed in this report, or develops others, or assigns duties to the counselor which vitiate counselor effectiveness if they are performed. It is the administrator, school principal or superintendent, who permits the counselor to work in distinctive ways or who uses him as a convenient administrative aid to perform countless chores which bear little relation to any acknowledged counselor function. Part of the unhappy situation that develops in many schools is the result of a lack of clarity upon the counselor's part, his inability to define clearly his professional responsibilities. Part is the principal's tendency to turn to a counselor for the easing of his own administrative load. If counselor and administrator could agree upon what the counselor must do to meet student and staff need in these changing times, a second responsibility of the administrator would be easier to handle.

This second responsibility is for the implicit assumptions about counselor responsibilities and standards of performance made by principals or superintendents when they employ counselors. Even more critical is the selection of staff who are encouraged to secure graduate education in this field as a prerequisite to assignment as counselors. Principals must seek those who have more than a desire to be helpful to students and who are liked by them — they must seek those who have a genuine respect for the dignity of students and who, in turn, are respected by as well as liked by students. *Nor should the rigid and inflexible person be employed,* no matter how "right" he may be, nor one who gives advice readily on all subjects. Nor the agreeable person who simply hasn't the desire or the ability to engage in graduate work.

A graduate faculty in counselor-education is frequently handicapped by the limited range of those who apply for graduate preparation in this field. To be sure the counselor-educator is responsible for establishing selection standards which reflect the standards of the graduate school as a whole as well as the particular requirements established for graduate students in this field. Their skirts are not clean for all too often they have failed to establish selection criteria which have been validated either academically or professionally.

School administrators and graduate faculty must confer on (1) *who is wanted on the job* and for what functions and (2) *who will succeed in graduate preparation* including supervised counseling experience. The administrator and the graduate teacher can each contribute significantly to the other if each will recognize what the other has to offer. The graduate school *is* responsible for standards of graduate work in this or any field but the knowledge of job conditions is equally essential. We are talking of preparation for a profession, and the preparation can be ahead of or tangential to the field only to a limited degree if frustration is not to result. An appropriate degree of "stretch" — of graduate standards that are in advance of field conditions — is desirable but stretch cannot be too great or it defeats itself. The graduate school teacher can learn from the administrator regarding the realism of school settings and demands. He can also contribute to the administrator's enlarged perception of changes in society and in counselor function.

*Professional Associations*

Such professional organizations as certain divisions of the American Personnel and Guidance Association and the American Psychological Association, the National Association of Secondary School Principals and the Association of Elementary School Principals are mutually concerned with counselor function and education. The principals' associations have responsibility for determining counselor function *with help* from the professional associations that are composed of counselors and counselor educators. The latter are concerned with setting standards for graduate school selection and education in this field *with help* from the principals on school realities, needs, and community conditions.

1. It is proposed that the two principals' associations study the proposals of this current report and make their own respective statement of changing counselor functions. It was by design and not by accident that the members of this Commission include a high school principal and a long-time school superintendent as well as social scientists, counselor administrators, and counselor educators. Their points of view, and those of other school administrators, have been sought and incorporated into this report. The task of presenting a forward look in counseling is truly a joint concern of social scientists, administrators, and counselors. But the *acceptance* of this perception of counselor function as indicative of future requirements, or the presentation of another picture of the future, is the responsibility of the principals' associations.

2. It is proposed that the American Personnel and Guidance Association, principally through the Association of Counselor Education and Supervision and the American School Counselor Association (two Divisions of the Association), and the American Psychological Association, principally through its Division of Counseling Psychology, jointly establish recommended standards for counselor education. This should include recommendations regarding the qualifications of both students who are admitted and the graduate staff who teach, the nature of the education provided, and the competencies expected of those who complete the program.

This type of broad-gauged planning is no dream of the future. As stated earlier in this chapter, a step forward in this direction was taken by the Executive Council of APGA in the summer of 1961 in a "position paper" that was given wide circulation. The two most concerned divisions of the association, those composed of counselor educators and school counselors, began in 1961, under the chairmanship of Willis E. Dugan, a more intensive grass-roots study of the specifics of counselor education which will be reported upon in 1962. A committee of the Division of Counseling Psychology of APA, under the chairmanship of Walter F. Johnson, reported out in 1961 a study of the special place of psychology in the education of counselors. Both APGA and APA committees included members of the current Commission on Guidance in American Schools.

3. It is proposed that state departments of education work in close collaboration with graduate schools in a periodic review of all counselor certification requirements. The certification of an individual must be for a limited time only and in like manner counselor certification requirements should be completely re-examined every three to five years. Both counselors and the requirements must keep pace with an accelerating rate of social, technological, and educational change. Immediate consideration should be given to the requirement of a block of graduate work in the social sciences, the requirement of supervised experience, and the requirement of a positive recommendation from the graduate school in which the student had his supervised counseling experience.

4. It is proposed that action follow the report of a nationwide study of the roles of pupil personnel and mental health workers in school and community currently being sponsored by a committee representing several national agencies. This will provide a clearer picture than we have had to date of the relationships existing between various types of professional and semi-professional workers. The appropriate professional associations should re-examine the role of the school counselor as soon as the comparative study becomes available. The current report is most certainly a projection into the future but it is far from the final word. There is no final word, now or ever. Change must follow change if the school counselor is to be responsive to the demands of an evolving culture.

## To the Counselor Now on the Job

The anticipation of a continuing education for all people in our rapidly expanding cultural universe applies with particular emphasis to those in professional fields of work. The school counselor has great need, and often a personally felt need, to continue to grow professionally and personally. Professor John R. Kinzer has written that the fundamentals in counseling are "the skills of communication, both written and oral; skill in interviewing; sensitivity to human feelings; knowledge of the

179

world; regard for human hopes and values; ability to lead others to understand themselves; understanding one's self; having, or at least developing, a philosophy of life; and, above all, intellectual honesty." These are qualities, both professional and personal, which one may continue to develop over a lifetime even though he well knows that he is not likely to reach complete fulfillment in any one of them.

The counseling institutes held under provisions of the 1958 National Defense Education Act provided new insights for thousands of counselors now in service as well as the beginning of professional education for others. (Approximately 9,000 were enrolled between the summer of 1959 and the school year 1961-1962). Counselors responded with particular enthusiasm to certain features of the varied graduate programs offered, such as better knowledge regarding the identification and motivation of talented students, exposure to current trends in the social sciences, supervision of practice in interviewing, and opportunity to engage in self-discovery.

From these and other sources it is possible to recommend:

1. That counselors now in schools consider professional updating as a continuous process lest they become fixated at one level of understanding and practice while the world of psychological and sociological thought and practice moves on and leaves them behind.

2. That school counselors include in their continuing professional education graduate courses and public lectures in the social and behavioral sciences, that they deliberately build an interdisciplinary approach into their graduate programs whether or not they are encouraged to do so by their advisers, that they systematically use professional meetings and reading to keep professionally alive.

3. That school counselors travel widely during the summers or vacation periods as a planned part of their attempt to understand other cultures and other peoples. Study of the culture and of the elements of the language in advance of the travel will not only make the travel itself more valuable but will contribute to a year-round experience of cultural broadening.

4. That school counselors study their own interviewing habits and attitudes and secure professional assistance in this process whenever possible. Personal study of taped interviews (always with the consent of the student interviewed and his awareness that this is for the counselor's own growth) is possible for almost anyone. The addition of another professional person in the process will contribute further insights whenever the counselor feels strong enough to want to see his interview through another's eyes. If the counselor can place himself as a learner under the

systematic supervision of a competent person, as in a graduate school setting, or with the assistance of a state or city supervisor, he will have the best opportunity to grow in interviewing effectiveness.

5. That the school counselor attempt to understand himself better through counseling or other professional help. This does not mean that he thinks of himself as other than normal but as a person who will gain in personal satisfaction and professional effectiveness if he has some improved insights into his own potential needs and defenses.

Psychologist Joseph Samler has said, "In a theory of creative mental health, nothing seems more stable than the idea that acceptance of and respect for others follows only from acceptance of and respect for oneself."

A school counselor put it differently as he evaluated the impact of a graduate course upon his own development:

> In terms of personal application, I feel that I am making progress in some of these areas. I may not, however, be fully sensitive of the position of others, especially those of a different background from my own, and I probably tend to project my own needs into the counseling situation. I feel that I may not have fully developed the "moral courage" necessary to face some of the difficult problems brought out in some of the case presentations. I feel that I may have difficulty communicating enthusiasm to the client, and that I am probably "wooden" in my approach. I probably will be somewhat defensive in cases where I lack counseling skill. Although I consider it a major concern, I do not consider myself fully conversant with my own religious and social values.
>
> This course has helped teach the importance of the relationship in the counseling process, and the importance of "caring." In relation to myself I feel most responsive to and understanding of others when my own needs are met and my personal life is in order. . . . In general, the material of this course has helped me to become aware of the need for the counselor's careful attention to his own mental hygiene.
>
> I have become vividly aware of the fact that a knowledge of the methods of individual and job appraisal are not sufficient for one to engage in the counseling process. Ability to understand the client's feelings and to communicate this understanding to him is of prime importance. . . . The whole matter of personal qualifications is a matter necessitating continuous appraisal and behavior modification. This course has helped to teach me that the counselor *himself* is a very important variable in the counseling process.

A superintendent of schools has said that "counselors should be persons who possess favorable qualities of being as well as technical competence." Some competencies can be sought through course work, others through supervised experience, but improvement of one's "favorable qualities of being" goes deeper. This, too, however, is a learning process and its outcome can be sought through self-understanding and creative self-expression. Mental health or personality health can often be best sought positively through understanding of the nature of one's personality needs and effective ways of satisfying them.

Maturity is not an unattainable ideal. *Maturity is the ability to live productively and with a sense of personal satisfaction in the regions of tension* between freedom and authority, between the rights of self and the rights of others, between the values one holds and what one does. One can *learn* to live maturely in these regions of tension, and he had better do so for it is of these regions that life is largely composed.

6. That school counselors give thoughtful attention to their purposes and goals as counselors. Some of what are deemed to be appropriate counseling goals have been stated elsewhere in this report. Does a given counselor accept these as his own and act accordingly or does he behave in terms of other goals? Can he specify these personally held goals?

One crucial decision regarding counseling goals must be made by every counselor: Am I a specialist for a few who are in trouble or am I a specialist for more with normal growth problems? The emphasis during the past decade or two upon psychology as the core of counselor education has been a mixed blessing. Such an emphasis has certainly focused upon the need for the school counselor to understand the student, and this has been essential. It has also led to a tendency for some counselors to be deeply concerned with the deviate student, with the emotionally disturbed, and with the student requiring intensive counseling. There is something fascinating in engaging in what is dangerously called psychotherapy. Counselors who do so are not always adequately prepared to counsel students with involved personality problems. Even if they were so prepared, they may have had to neglect the normal developmental needs of other students because of the time taken by the troubled student.

The outcome of this state of affairs has been a confused public image of the school counselor. Is he a counselor of the healthy or a psychotherapist of the ill? Or is he simply a purveyor of information about schools and jobs? There is no question but that a well-prepared counselor can be an effective worker with an emotionally disturbed student, at least the most effective one available. If he has adequate training and the requisite personal qualities, he may well be an invaluable resource person for teachers and principals who are faced with "problem students." The temptation to have the counselor deal extensively with such individuals has, however, meant the loss of his services to many other students whose developmental needs may have been equally urgent and whose contribution to society may be even greater.

Sound psychological training is essential, and there probably cannot be too much of it, but it seems desirable to place the focus upon the developmental and preventive rather than upon the curative and remedial. That a minority of students need intensive professional help there is little question. That the counselor should take his valuable insights and skills away from the great body of students who have possibilities of becoming more effective and creative individuals because of the counselor's assistance and give them to the few seems a doubtful use of counseling talent. With commendable sincerity but a thoughtless division of time too many counselors year after year cultivate and seek normal growth in rocky soil while ignoring vast areas of rich soil which could yield superior results.[2]

Another goal problem is the counselor's decision that he really *wants* the more demanding professional emphasis in his daily work. The counselor is not free from the temptation to "escape into" the very routine duties of which he is critical. Dr. Seyler, Deputy Superintendent of Schools in Los Angeles, recently gave this warning to an audience of counselors. "Please be sure that you do not enjoy routine, clerical duties. Please be sure that as more clerical time is assigned that more of these routine duties *are* given to the clerical staff. Just be sure that you are not guilty of escaping into routine." A survey of high school counselors in a large city system was critical of the large proportion of time spent by counselors in schedule planning of a rather routine nature. But, the report authors state, some of the counselors enjoy this routine work and draw it to themselves. In general these were not the highest rated counselors in the system or the best educated. The counselor may select a routine goal or a demanding one. His goal selection and goal acceptance

---

[2] Dugald Arbuckle registers a dissent to most of what has been written thus far under item 6. He proposes that counselors are more likely to neglect problems of feelings and emotions and believes that a concern for these areas is an appropriate emphasis in school counseling. The writer would not disagree in kind, certainly for the adequately prepared counselor. The disagreement is one of degree and emphasis. He would clarify the image in a different manner from that proposed by Dr. Arbuckle.

affects markedly what the administrator accepts as "right" for the counselor.

7. Closely related to goals are the counselor's personal values. There is evidence that these cannot be concealed from the client even though there is no verbal communication of them. What the counselor considers important is communicated in all sorts of subtle ways. It is important that the counselor be explicitly aware of his convictions for these may color his appraisal of a student and color also the counselor's perception of the student that is communicated to him. That one's ethics are based upon the values that one accepts as appropriate to one's self seems also an unassailable conclusion. For the counselor to engage in self-study and in discussion with others of his own deeply held convictions and ethical concepts could result in greater personal insights and better counseling relationships.

8. That the school counselor study the programming of computers (a "program" is the sequences of items to be inserted into the computer that will result in machine calculation of the desired answers) and be able to develop programs for his own informational needs. Electronic computers will be increasingly a part of every school system and they need to be used 24 hours a day in order to justify the cost. The counselor "of the future" needs to know how to utilize the speed and accuracy of the computer to secure information that is needed in carrying out his counseling function in the school.

Such a counselor should also understand the learning principles involved in the use of self-teaching devices (teaching machines and programmed textbooks.) Widespread use of these units is projected but also much misunderstanding of their function by both teachers and students. As one of the school staff with more psychological sophistication than most of the teachers, the counselor should be familiar with the learning principles that are involved and with the justification of such units in the school's instructional program. This does not mean that he needs to defend them but to understand them as devices designed to carry psychological principles into practice.

9. That the counselor develop a program for living in a personally satisfying manner. He needs concerts, reading, travel, and stimulating companionship if he is to become, or to remain, a person who is interesting to students and to colleagues. He needs a reservoir of deep emotional and spiritual experiences to draw upon. He must not feed his head alone, but also his heart and his spirit. Recently the Danforth Foundation began requiring its fellows to submit a budget for "cultural activities" along with the budget for food, shelter, tuition, etc. It would

be well for every counselor to build in a personal budget dedicated to improving the quality of his personal living and being.

Paul Tillich has said that this generation suffers because it has lost the dimension of depth. We range over a wide field in our attempts to keep up but probe deeply at very few points. To Tillich this lost dimension is the sense of constant query — "Why am I here — What is my purpose — Whence am I headed?" — a continuing search for the meaning of life. That we never find it completely is disturbing but it need not be. It is important only that we constantly *search* and become changed in the process of searching.

Counselors, as students of people and their lives, should be searchers, should be conscious of the dimension of depth. The search may lead us anywhere — truth and beauty found through art, science, philosophy, religion. We have good precedent. Einstein was and Schweitzer is a constant searcher. Einstein said that to find a satisfying answer to the meaning of life "means to be religious." What does it mean to be religious? Schweitzer said that the secret of life is "reverence for life." What is the meaning of reverence?

10. That the counselor take pride in his work and have joy in the doing. The communication of this satisfaction to the student may be one of the counselor's most effective contributions. No one has said it better than Kahlil Gibran in *The Prophet*:

> Work is love made visible.
>
> And if you cannot work with love but only with distaste, it is better that you should leave your work and sit at the gate of the temple and take alms of those who work with joy.
>
> For if you bake bread with indifference, you bake a bitter bread that feeds but half a man's hunger.[3]

Students deserve more than bitter bread.

[3] Reprinted from *The Prophet* by Kahlil Gibran with permission of the publisher, Alfred A. Knopf, Inc. Copyright 1923 by Kahlil Gibran; renewal copyright 1951 by Administrators C. T. A. of Kahlil Gibran Estate, and Mary G. Gibran.

# Acknowledgments

Since this study has attempted to project change in several dimensions of society, a great many people were consulted. Panels of social scientists were convened at several places in the country, panels of educators in other places. Individuals by the score were asked to check on tentative projections, were asked to dream a little with the writer. Without attempting a complete listing, which means that some most helpful people will be inadvertently omitted, the writer's debt to the following is hereby acknowledged.

*In the social sciences:*

Dr. Joseph Bobbitt, National Institute of Mental Health; Dr. Herbert Streiner, Brookings Institution; Dr. Henry Rieken, National Science Foundation; Dr. Philip Davison, RAND Corporation; Dr. Donald Michael, formerly of Brookings Institution, now with the Peace Research Institute; Dr. Dewey Anderson, Public Affairs Institute; Dr. Don Paarlberg, President's Council of Economic Advisors; Dr. Reinhard Bendix, Dr. Seymour Lippsett, Dr. Martin Trow, Dr. Jack London, Dr. William Peterson, all of the Sociology Department of the University of California; Dr. William Sewell, University of Wisconsin; Dr. Albert Rees, University of Chicago; Dean Russell Cooper and the planning staff of deans of the new University of South Florida.

*In psychology and its application to counseling:*

Dr. Howard Hunt, University of Chicago; Dr. Carl Rogers, University of Wisconsin; Dr. Theodore Newcomb, University of Michigan; Dr. Fritz Redl, Wayne State University; Dr. Robert Mathewson, The University of the City of New York; Dr. Ben Bloom, University of Chicago; Dr. Robert Pace, then of Syracuse University; many of my colleagues of the University of Minnesota, particularly Dr. Willis Dugan.

*In educational change and its implications for counseling:*

Panels of professors of education at University of Missouri (Dr. Robert Callis, chairman), University of Colorado (Dr. Clifford Houston, chairman), the City University of New York (Dr. Robert Mathewson, chairman), University of California (Dr. Lawrence Stewart, chairman), University of Minnesota (Dr. Willis Dugan, chairman); Dr. Hugh Bell and Dr. Clarence Mahler, Chico State College; the 32 counselor educators who made extensive contributions to my thinking on the education of counselors.

There are a few individuals to whom an even greater personal debt of direct assistance, encouragement, and painstaking support is hereby acknowledged:

Dr. Arthur A. Hitchcock, Executive Director of the American Personnel and Guidance Association, Mr. Carl McDaniels, and others of the Association staff.

Dr. Dael Wolfle, Chairman of the Commission, and *each member* of the Commission.

186

Mr. John Pfeiffer, professional science writer, New Hope, Pennsylvania.

Mr. John Gardner, President of the Carnegie Corporation.

Dr. John C. Flanagan, Dr. John T. Dailey, and Dr. Isadore Goldberg for cooperation in the use of Project TALENT data.

Dr. Richard H. Byrne, Professor of Education, University of Maryland.

Officers of the American School Counselor Association, the most recent being Mr. G. William Murphy, President during 1961–1962.

None of these individuals should be held responsible for anything in the report. The responsibility is wholly mine, but I am at the same time deeply grateful to them for many substantial forward thrusts and many stern admonitions on the appropriate turning of a phrase.

C. GILBERT WRENN

# A Selected List of
# Written Sources of Information

## Social Change

Brown, Harrison, Bonner, James, and Weir, John. *The Next Hundred Years*, Viking Press, 1958.

The Corporation for Economic and Industrial Research. *World-Wide and Domestic Economic Problems and Their Impact on the Foreign Policy of the United States*, prepared for the U. S. Senate Committee on Foreign Relations, 1959.

Drucker, Peter F. *America's Next 20 Years*, Harper, 1957.

Drucker, Peter F. *Landmarks of Tomorrow*, Harper, 1959.

Ginzberg, Eli (Ed.). *The Nation's Children:* Volume 1, *The Family and Social Change*, White House Conference on Children and Youth, 1960.

Jarrett, Henry (Ed.). *Science and Resources, Prospects and Implications of Technological Advance*, Johns Hopkins, 1959.

Joint Committee on Atomic Energy. *Engineering and Scientific Manpower in the U. S., Western Europe, and Russia,* prepared for the U. S. Senate Committee on Foreign Relations, 1959.

The National Planning Association. *Long-Range Projections for Economic Growth, The American Economy in 1970*, Washington, D. C., 1959.

Stanford Research Institute. *Possible Non-Military Scientific Developments and Their Potential Impact on Foreign Policy Problems of the United States*, prepared for the U. S. Senate Committee on Foreign Relations, 1959.

Thruelson, Richard, and Kobler, John (Eds.). *Adventures of the Mind*, Knopf, 1960.

## Educational Change

Brandwein, Paul F. *The Gifted Student As Future Scientist*, Harcourt Brace, 1955.

Bruner, Jerome S. *The Process of Education*, Harvard University Press, 1960.

College Entrance Examination Board. *The Search for Talent*, Educational Testing Service, Princeton, N. J., 1960.

College Entrance Examination Board. *Counseling in School and College*, Educational Testing Service, Princeton, N. J., 1961.

Coleman, James S. *Social Climates in High Schools*, U. S. Office of Education, 1961.

*Education Supplements of the Saturday Review*, starting with September 17, 1960, and monthly since then. Paul Woodring, editor. Sponsored by the Ford Fund for the Advancement of Education.

Gardner, John W. *From High School to Job. How To Think About College.* From 1960 and 1957 Annual Reports of the Carnegie Corporation of New York (available from the Corporation as reprints).

Journal of the National Association of Women Deans and Counselors. *New Programs and Procedures in High School,* Volume 24, October, 1960.

President's Commission on National Goals. *Goals for Americans,* Prentice Hall, 1960.

Special Studies Project V of the Rockefeller Brothers Fund. *The Pursuit of Excellence: Education and the Future of America,* Doubleday and Co., 1958.

Trump, F. Lloyd. *Images of the Future,* National Association of Secondary School Principals, 1959.

## Psychological Thought and Counseling Purpose

Allport, G. W. *Becoming,* Yale University Press, 1955.

Erickson, E. H. *Childhood and Society,* Norton, 1950.

Goldman, Leo. *Using Tests in Counseling,* Appleton-Century-Crofts, 1961.

Horney, K. *The Neurotic Personality of Our Time,* Norton, 1937.

Mathewson, R. H. *Guidance Policy and Practice* (rev. ed.), Harper, 1955.

May, Rollo, *et al. Existence,* Basic Books, 1959.

Miller, C. H. *Foundations of Guidance,* Harper, 1961.

Rogers, Carl R. *On Becoming a Person,* Houghton Mifflin, 1961.

Skinner, B. P. *Science and Human Behavior,* Macmillan, 1953.

Super, Donald E. *Psychology of Careers,* Harper, 1957.

Wheelis, A. *The Quest for Identity,* Norton, 1958.

Tables Which Present Data
From the Three Studies of Counselors

TABLE 1

Information about the Counselor from Three Studies of Counselors

| | ASCA Member Counselors (N = 242) | Project TALENT Counselors (N = 786) | Elementary School Counselors (N = 138) |
|---|---|---|---|
| Sex | 54% male | 61% male | 31% male |
| Median Age | 43 | 40 | 44 |
| Masters Degree | 89% | 70% | 60% |
| Size of School | 50% in schools over 1,000 enrollment | 13% in schools with graduating classes over 400<br><br>44% with graduating classes under 100 | 58% in schools of 500–1,000 enrollment |
| Type of School | 50% in 3-4 yr. Sr. H.S.<br>22% Jr. H.S.<br>18% 6-yr. H.S. | 57% in 3–4 yr. Sr. H.S.<br>21% 6 yr. H.S.<br>22% K-12 schools | 76% in grades 1–6 |
| Number of Students for Whom Responsible | Median of 412 | ——— | Median of 690[b] |
| Titles Used | Counselor—40%<br>Guid. Dir.—30%<br>Guid. Coun.—17% | ——— | Counselor—39%<br>Elem. Guid. Coun.—22% |
| Proportion of Time Assigned to Guidance Program | 73% full-time<br>20% half-time or more | 20% full-time<br>55% half-time or more | 98% full-time<br>2% half-time or more |
| Proportion of Time Counseling Students (Full-time Counselors Only) | 35% half-time or more<br>63% 3 periods daily | ——— | 25% half-time or more<br>55% 3 periods daily |
| Consulting with Teachers and Parents | 30% 2 periods or more daily | ——— | 55% 2 periods or more daily |
| Group Work with Students | 70% 1–2 periods daily | ——— | 57% 1–2 periods daily |
| Program Mechanics and Clerical Work | 74% 1–2 periods daily | ——— | 75% 1–2 periods daily |

[a] Roughly comparable information from: (1) the Study of Members of the American School Counselor Association (91% response from a 10% random sample); (2) the Project TALENT Study of counselors (93% response from a 5% random sample of schools); and (3) the Elementary School Counselors Study (71% response from counselors in selected areas). All data were collected in the spring of 1960.

[b] It should be kept in mind that 36% of the elementary school counselors of this study served in more than one school (28% in a 2 or 3 school situation).

TABLE 2

Proportions of All Guidance Periods
And Individual Interview Periods
Per Day by Size of Schools
And Number of Counselors
(Approximated Figures from the TALENT Study)

| Size of Graduating Class | Ratio of Counselor to School | Average Number of Periods Per Counselor Per Day for All Guidance Work | Average Number of Periods Per Counselor Per Day for Individual Interviewing |
|---|---|---|---|
| 0–24 | 1 : 2.3 | 3.6 | 2.0 |
| 25–99 | 1 : 1.5 | 4.3 | 2.7 |
| 100–399 | 2.3 : 1 | 5.6 | 3.7 |
| Over 400 | 5 : 1 | 5.5 | 3.5 |
| All Schools | 1 : 1 | 4.8 | 2.8 |

# TABLE 3

Responses of Members of the American School Counselor Association and Counselors in the Elementary School Counselors Study to Questions about Present and Future Functions of the Counselor

|  | Secondary (N = 242) | Elementary (N = 138) |
|---|---|---|
|  | Per cent of counselors whose responses fell into these categories | |

I. *Basic activities to be maintained in the future*

| | | |
|---|---|---|
| 1. Counseling students (developmental, educational, vocational, personal, etc.) | **100**[a][b] | 71[a] |
| 2. Conferences with groups of parents and counseling individual parents | 45 | **65** |
| 3. Test administration and interpretation | 41 | 33 |
| 4. Conferences with a teacher or teachers, counseling a teacher | 37 | **63** |
| 5. Student group guidance and orientation | **32** | 13 |
| 6. Evaluation, follow-up, research | **16** | 3 |
| 7. Referrals to and contact with community agencies | 16 | 24 |
| 8. Vocational information, collection and dissemination, contacts with employers, etc. | **12** | 0 |
| 9. Involvement in curriculum development | 8 | 6 |

II. *Present activities that are not the duties of a counselor (should not be maintained)*

| | | |
|---|---|---|
| 1. Nothing is wrong (or omits any response to item) | 17 | **35** |
| 2. Clerical work (checking records, filing, preparing transcripts, etc.) | **50** | 24 |
| 3. Supervises study hall, lunch room, library, roll room, etc. | 32 | 30 |
| 4. Routine discipline not involving counseling | 20 | 14 |
| 5. Psychometrist duties (scoring, recording, etc.) | 20 | 18 |
| 6. Duties normally those of teachers (grade reports, class schedules, etc.) | 15 | 10 |
| 7. Working on school schedule | **15** | 1 |
| 8. Class sponsorship, student activities | 15 | 16 |
| 9. Teaching | 7 | 13 |

[a] A given counselor may have listed more than one kind of counseling activity under this heading so that the total number of responses may not represent exactly 100 per cent of the counselors. The total number of responses for all counseling categories was 466.

[b] The boldface type highlights an item contributed by an appreciably larger proportion of one group than the other. No tests of significance of the difference have been applied.

# TABLE 4

Recommendations Regarding Emphasis in Counselor Preparation for the Future from Members of ASCA and Members of the Elementary School Counselor Study

|  | Secondary (N = 242) % | Elementary (N = 138) % |
|---|---|---|
| *More Course Work Preparation in:* | | |
| Psychology | 54 | 29 |
| Practicum, internship, etc. | 23 | 22 |
| Tests and Measurements | 14 | 16 |
| Counseling Techniques | 17 | 29 |
| Vocational Information | 11 | — |
| Personality Development and Developmental Psychology | 9 | 32 |
| Knowledge of School-Community Relations | — | 16 |
| Sociology and Economics | 11 | 12 |
| Clinical Case Studies | — | 9 |
| Statistics and Research | 7 | — |
| Educational Curriculum and Philosophy | 6 | — |
| *Other Than Course Work:* | | |
| Teaching Experience | 12 | 7 |
| Non-Teaching Work Experience | 10 | — |
| Broad Cultural, Values, Background | 12 | 6 |
| Group Work and Group Dynamic Skills | 8 | 10 |

Southern Christian University Library
1200 Taylor Rd.
Montgomery, AL. 36117